Religions
of the World

# Mormonism

Corinne J. Naden and Rose Blue

LUCENT
BOOKS®

THOMSON

GALE

San Diego • Detroit • New York • San Francisco • Cleveland • New Haven, Conn. • Waterville, Maine • London • Munich

On cover: A fanfare of trumpets opens a performance of the annual
Mormon Pageant staged on Hill Cumorah, near Palmyra, New York.

© 2004 by Lucent Books. Lucent Books is an imprint of The Gale Group, Inc.,
a division of Thomson Learning, Inc.

Lucent Books® and Thomson Learning™ are trademarks used herein under license.

*For more information, contact*
Lucent Books
27500 Drake Rd.
Farmington Hills, MI 48331-3535
Or you can visit our Internet site at http://www.gale.com

**LIBRARY OF CONGRESS CATALOGING-IN-PUBLICATION DATA**

Naden, Corinne J.
  Mormonism / by Corinne J. Naden and Rose Blue.
    v. cm. — (Religions of the world)
Includes bibliographical references and index.
Contents: Mormonism: mystery and reality—Joseph Smith and the origins of
Mormonism—Mormon doctrines—Building the Church—Brigham Young and the trek to
Deseret—Mormonism today—Spreading the word—The Mormon message: in this world
and of this world.
  ISBN 1-59018-452-1
  1. Mormon Church. [1. Mormon Church.] I. Blue, Rose. II. Title. III. Religions of the world
(San Diego, Calif.)
  BX8611.N34 2004
  289.3—dc22
                                                                      2003017110

Printed in the United States of America

# Contents

Foreword     4

Introduction     Mormonism: Mystery and Reality     6

Chapter 1     Joseph Smith and the Origins of
Mormonism     9

Chapter 2     Mormon Doctrines     22

Chapter 3     Building the Church     37

Chapter 4     Brigham Young and the Trek to Deseret     52

Chapter 5     Mormonism Today     67

Chapter 6     Spreading the Word     84

Epilogue     The Morman Message: In This World
and of This World     98

Notes     100

For Further Reading     102

Works Consulted     103

Index     105

Picture Credits     111

About the Authors     112

# Foreword

Religion has always been a central component of human culture, though its form and practice have changed through time. Ancient people lived in a world they could not explain or comprehend. Their world consisted of an environment controlled by vague and mysterious powers attributed to a wide array of gods. Artifacts dating to a time before recorded history suggest that the religion of the distant past reflected this world, consisting mainly of rituals devised to influence events under the control of these gods.

The steady advancement of human societies brought about changes in religion as in all other things. Through time, religion came to be seen as a system of beliefs and practices that gave meaning to—or allowed acceptance of—anything that transcended the natural or the known. And, the belief in many gods ultimately was replaced in many cultures by the belief in a Supreme Being.

As in the distant past, however, religion still provides answers to timeless questions: How, why, and by whom was the universe created? What is the ultimate meaning of human life? Why is life inevitably followed by death? Does the human soul continue to exist after death, and if so, in what form? Why is there pain and suffering in the world, and why is there evil?

In addition, all the major world religions provide their followers with a concrete and clearly stated ethical code. They offer a set of moral instructions, defining virtue and evil and what is required to achieve goodness. One of these universal moral codes is compassion toward others above all else. Thus, Judaism, Christianity, Islam, Hinduism, Buddhism, Confucianism, and Taoism each teach a version of the so-called golden rule, or in the words of Jesus Christ, "As ye would that men should do to you, do ye also to them likewise" (Luke 6:31). For example, Confucius instructed his disciples to "never impose on others what you would not choose for yourself" (*Analects:* 12:2). The Hindu epic poem,

Mahabharata, identifies the core of all Hindu teaching as not doing unto others what you do not wish done to yourself. Similarly Muhammad declared that no Muslim could be a true believer unless he desires for his brother no less than that which he desires for himself.

It is ironic, then, that although compassionate concern for others forms the heart of all the major religions' moral teachings, religion has also been at the root of countless conflicts throughout history. It has been suggested that much of the appeal that religions hold for humankind lies in their unswerving faith in the truth of their particular vision. Throughout history, most religions have shared a profound confidence that their interpretation of life, God, and the universe is the right one, thus giving their followers a sense of certainty in an uncertain and often fragile existence. Given the assurance displayed by most religions regarding the fundamental correctness of their teachings and practices, it is perhaps not surprising that religious intolerance has fueled disputes and even full-scale wars between peoples and nations time and time again, from the Crusades of medieval times to the current bloodshed in Northern Ireland and the Middle East.

Today, as violent religious conflicts trouble many parts of our world, it has become more important than ever to learn about the similarities as well as the differences between faiths. One of the most effective ways to accomplish this is by examining the beliefs, customs, and values of various religions. In the Religions of the World series, students will find a clear description of the core creeds, rituals, ethical teachings, and sacred texts of the world's major religions. In-depth explorations of how these faiths changed over time, how they have influenced the social customs, laws, and education of the countries in which they are practiced, and the particular challenges each one faces in coming years are also featured.

Extensive quotations from primary source materials, especially the core scriptures of each faith, and a generous number of secondary source quotations from the works of respected modern scholars are included in each volume in the series. It is hoped that by gaining insight into the faiths of other peoples and nations, students will not only gain a deeper appreciation and respect for different religious beliefs and practices, but will also gain new perspectives on and understanding of their own religious traditions.

# Mormonism: Mystery and Reality

Mormonism, formally known as the Church of Jesus Christ of Latter-day Saints (LDS), is a religion of mystery to many Americans. While most people know that its headquarters are in Salt Lake City, Utah, and that the Mormon Tabernacle Choir sings there, most know very little about the people who call themselves Mormons. Followers of this religion believe that the Book of Mormon, written by its founder, Joseph Smith Jr., is the word of God.

Part of the mystery that surrounds this religion is fostered by the Mormons themselves. Mormons call themselves the "peculiar people" and embrace the term as a badge of honor representing their status as God's chosen ones. They say that they are "in" this world but not "of" this world and believe that God has set them apart from all others. The term "peculiar people" also refers to their pride in their ancestors, who endured persecution for their beliefs.

The beliefs and practices of the Mormon faith often seem mysterious to outsiders. Unlike other Christians, Mormons believe that God was once a man and that men can become gods. They also believe that Jesus of Nazareth visited the New World after his resurrection. Mormons are secure in the knowledge that families can be reunited after death and that baptism for those already dead can allow them to enter the celestial kingdom.

## The Spreading Faith

Despite the air of mystery that surrounds the Church of Latter-day Saints, it is one of the fastest growing religions in the world. There are more than 5 million Mormons in the United States and more than 11 million worldwide. About 65 percent of the people who live in Salt Lake City belong to the Mormon Church; about 70 percent of the people who live in the state of Utah are Mormons. And their numbers are growing. Membership has doubled in the United States since the 1950s, making Mormonism the nation's sixth-largest religious denomination.

The increase in membership worldwide has been even more spectacular. By the early twenty-first century, some fifty-nine thousand Mormon missionaries were working in 119

*A statue of Brigham Young stands near the Mormon temple in Salt Lake City. Young led his followers to Utah in 1847, where today 70 percent of the population is Mormon.*

*Elder Edwin Q. Cannon Jr., a Mormon missionary, baptizes Nigerian converts. Mormon missionaries seek converts all over the world.*

countries around the world. Largely through their work, the worldwide Mormon population now numbers about 11 million. They are dedicated to spreading the gospel that the Church of Jesus Christ of Latter-day Saints is the one and only true church. It is this kind of dedication that some statisticians say will double membership in the church by 2010. This is a startling increase to non-Mormons, for whom the Mormon Church remains so much a mystery.

In addition to its growing population, the Mormon Church is wealthy. Its estimated worth is roughly $10 billion. Its wealth gives it great power in its mission to spread the gospel.

Mormons believe that it is their destiny to convert nonbelievers to Mormonism, which they are certain is the true religion. To understand their commitment, it is necessary to understand the beginnings of these "peculiar people" and what is essentially a truly American church. To understand the depth of their crusade, it is necessary to look beyond the mystery into the history and the lives of the Latter-day Saints.

# chapter one

# Joseph Smith and the Origins of Mormonism

Joseph Smith founded the Church of Jesus Christ of Latter-day Saints, claiming direct contact with God and asserting the faith to be the one and only true religion. These beliefs became the solid foundation and enduring strength of Mormonism. They are also the source of its lingering persecution by others.

Smith, the first prophet and spiritual leader of the Mormons, did not claim to have started a new religion; but rather he claimed to have restored the true religion of the Bible. He was not a learned man in the manner of religious leaders such as John Calvin or Martin Luther. He did not try to find a different message in the Bible as a breaking-away or starting-off point for something else. Smith said that his message came directly from God. Because of Smith's claim, followers of the Church of Jesus Christ of Latter-day Saints regard him as their prophet and their leader.

## A Revivalist Background

Smith was born on a rented farm in Sharon, Vermont, on December 23, 1805. The early 1800s was a period of intense revivalism, or religious fervor, in New England. During this so-called Great Awakening (1795–1835), Protestant leaders sought both to revitalize the spiritual feelings of their members and to win converts. Winning new souls became the primary function of the ministry, with renewed emphasis on local prayer meetings and moral living.

Joseph Smith Jr. was born into this atmosphere, in which divination and mysticism were common. Divination is a method of telling the future by ways such as interpreting dreams or reading cards. Mysticism involves a search for hidden truth or wisdom.

His parents, Joseph Smith Sr. and Lucy Mack Smith, were constantly searching for religious truth or wisdom. Devout Christians with strong beliefs, they could not feel comfortable among organized churches. Joseph's mother attended several Methodist revival meetings in her search for spiritual salvation; his father believed in the Bible and in folk magic. However, by the time Joseph was born, the elder Smith had decided that no one religion understood more about the kingdom of God than any other.

Joseph was the fourth of eight surviving Smith children (two other siblings died in infancy). He was five years old when the family moved to Lebanon, New Hampshire, in 1811. Although the three oldest children

*Claiming to be the direct messenger of God, Joseph Smith established the Mormon Church in 1829.*

were sent to public school for the first time, it is not known whether Joseph ever attended school or was solely taught at home. What is known is that he did learn to read and write.

## The Illness

In 1812 Joseph contracted typhoid fever. While many died in the epidemic that swept the town, Joseph recovered in two weeks. However, soon after his recovery he suddenly experienced severe shoulder pain. The doctor found a large sore in the boy's armpit that he opened and drained, but the pain moved to Joseph's left leg, which became infected and began to swell. Over the next several weeks, the boy suffered great pain from infection and swelling. Other doctors diagnosed the problem as osteomyelitis, a bacterial infection of the bone. Because doctors had almost no knowledge of what caused infection, much less how to cure it, in those days, there was little that could be done. The doctors wanted to amputate the boy's leg, but mother and son both refused.

According to his mother, Joseph not only refused to allow the amputation, but he also refused any anesthesia while the doctors drilled through his leg to remove the diseased bone, which shortened the leg slightly. Joseph endured several more months of painful recovery and was left with a permanent limp.

The revivalist atmosphere was still strong when the Smith family moved to Palmyra, New York, a small town bordering the Erie Canal, in 1816. Joseph occasionally attended the Presbyterian church there with his

*Revivalist meetings like this one were popular in New England at the time of Joseph Smith's birth. Preachers at such meetings tried to inspire religious fervor in order to win converts.*

mother. Joseph's father still refused to go to church, declaring that it was full of hypocrites. This atmosphere of revivalism in the community, coupled with strong beliefs but antichurch feelings at home, apparently caused some confusion about religion for eleven-year-old Joseph.

Joseph Smith's mother described her son as a quiet boy who was not very interested in books but was often deep in meditation. Like his father, Joseph noted that many who professed deep faith failed to live according to their stated beliefs. Mormon historian Richard L. Bushman draws this picture:

> To others who knew him less well, Joseph seemed slow, "destitute of genius," but between twelve and fifteen he seriously searched the scriptures, "believing as I was taught that they contained the word of God." He was confused by the failings of the Christians in the town. . . . "This was a grief to my Soul." . . . The failings of the church people made him wonder where salvation was to be found and forced him to search.[1]

## The Visitations

Confusion about religion and about which church spoke the truth led Joseph Smith to a private decision when he was fourteen years old. He would appeal directly to God for guidance to find the path to true salvation. On an early spring morning in 1820, he went into the woods near the family cabin and began to pray for help. In Smith's own words:

> I retired to a secret place in a grove and began to call upon the Lord. . . . I was enwrapped in a heavenly vision and saw two glorious personages who exactly resembled each other in features and likeness, surrounded with a brilliant light which eclipsed the sun at noonday. They told me that all religious denominations were believing in incorrect doctrines and that none of them was acknowledged of God as his church and kingdom. And I was expressly commanded to "go not after them," at the same time receiving a promise that the fulness of the gospel should at some future time be made known unto me.[2]

This was later called the First Vision, although at the time Smith did not think of it as such. In fact, he did not know what to think of it and did not tell his parents of the experience. He did, however, tell a local minister about it. The minister was highly skeptical. It was not unusual

# The Mother of the Prophet

Joseph Smith Jr. was born to a dreamer father who flitted from place to place and job to job, but it was his mother, Lucy Mack Smith, who was the motivating force in his life. She was an energetic, forceful woman who believed in signs, miracles, visions, and charms, just as her own father had. Beset by misfortune throughout her life, she nevertheless took charge whenever a calamity occurred. Shortly before young Joseph came down with a fever in 1812, his older sister Sophronia fell ill with typhoid. After a ninety-day siege, the young girl was still alive but limp and motionless. Mother and father sat near her bed helpless. Suddenly, Lucy jumped up, wrapped the girl in a blanket, and began to pace the floor. She did so until Sophronia began to cry. The fever was broken.

Lucy was proud of her part in curing her daughter and, later, in the decision not to amputate young Joseph's leg. But the great misfortune of her life was the loss of three sons, which she faced not with sorrow but with anger. Joseph and Hyrum were assassinated, and Samuel died of a fever. All these happenings in the Smith family are known only through Lucy. She was the only one—including Joseph Jr.— in the family to leave an account of Smith history. She wrote *Biographical Sketches of Joseph Smith, the Prophet, and His Progenitors for Many Generations,* first published in 1853. It contains most of what is known of the Prophet's early years, even though his mother does not mention his name until page 56.

in this time of religious fervor for children to report visions and divine appearances. What most concerned the minister was Smith's assertion that all the established churches were wrong; that none held the rightful place in God's kingdom.

As moving as Smith later recalled the First Vision to be, in the immediate aftermath life went on much as before. He worked on his father's farm and said little about his spiri-

tual feelings, although he remembered the vision. By 1823 Smith, now seventeen years old, was a tall, pleasant young man with a friendly smile and arresting blue eyes. As he said later, he was concerned that he spent too much time in lighthearted behavior and not enough in serious thought. He began to worry again about his state of salvation.

On the evening of Sunday, September 21, 1823, when the rest of the family had gone to sleep in the crowded home, Smith began to ask God's forgiveness because he was not more devout. He later reported that the room grew bright until it was like daylight. Suddenly in front of him was a figure suspended in the air and clad in white. Smith would later write, "He had on a loose robe of most exquisite whiteness. It was a whiteness beyond anything earthly I had ever seen; nor do I believe that any earthly thing could be made to appear so exceedingly white and brilliant."[3]

The apparition in white announced itself as Moroni, messenger of God, and said that God had work for Smith to do. It was work unlike any other and would cause Smith's name to be both praised and cursed. Moroni then told Smith of a book written on gold plates that were stored in a box. The book—which would later be known as the Book of Mormon—told of the former early inhabitants of the Americas. In addition to the book, there were two stones (called Urim and Thummim) that were wrapped in silver bows and fastened to a breastplate. They were known as seer-stones and would aid in the translation of the plates. Smith understood that he was to locate the plates, translate them, and prepare for the return of Christ to earth.

Moroni warned Smith against showing the plates or the stones to anyone else until a later date, and then only to those designated to see them. To disobey, Moroni said, would mean Smith's destruction. The messenger Moroni appeared two more times to Smith that night, the last time warning him against the temptations of Satan.

The next morning Smith's father commented on his son's shaken appearance, but Smith said nothing. However, when the boy fainted while working in the field, Moroni appeared again and urged him to tell his father of the vision. Smith told his father, who believed him (perhaps because the elder Smith also believed in visions) and instructed the boy to obey the messenger.

## Finding the Plates

Shortly after Moroni's visit, Smith went to a hill about three miles from the family farm, which his vision had indicated as the place where the plates were buried. There, under a large rock, he found the plates in a stone box. Moroni had warned that although he was not yet mature enough spiritually to take custody of them, he must make periodic visits to the site. Moroni also warned Smith against trying to profit from the plates by selling them or by using

*In one of Joseph Smith's visions, God's messenger Moroni reveals the location of the golden plates on which the text of the Book of Mormon is written.*

the money to pay off the mortgage on the family farm.

Smith returned to the site many times during the next few years. In 1826, at his father's insistence, the two set out on a treasure-hunting expedition near the town of Harmony, Pennsylvania. Smith Sr. was convinced that they would find treasure in the area, but they did not find anything. However, young Smith met Emma Hale in the house where the two men boarded while looking for treasure, and he and Emma were attracted to each other. Although her father viewed Joseph as a fortune hunter, Hale's disapproval did not stop Emma from marrying Joseph in January 1827. The couple was deeply devoted, and she later became very involved in her husband's mission.

On September 27, 1827, Smith returned to the hill and was given custody of the plates. They were described as thin, golden sheets bound with three golden rings. Moroni warned Smith to never let them out of his care. Smith also found a peculiar pair of eyeglasses—two translucent stones set in silver frames connected to each other. These were the seer-stones, Urim and Thummim, which would aid in translating the plates.

Smith returned to the family home with the plates but was concerned about their safety. Despite family secrecy, and quite likely because his father had mentioned the plates to a friend, the rumor of their existence soon spread. Smith realized he could not begin the translation in peace and safety, and he and his wife moved back to Harmony. Emma's father, who was now more accepting of the marriage, gave them a few acres of land, and the couple moved into a small cabin on the site. There Smith began the translation of the Book of Mormon.

## The Book of Mormon

Smith later said that the gold plates were covered with what he called reformed Egyptian lettering. When he looked at them through the seer-stones, the English translation of the words became clear to him. Smith later claimed that "through the medium of the Urim and Thummim I translated the record by the gift, and power of God."[4]

This was quite astonishing to his wife, as quoted by biographer Robert Remini: "No man could have done it, she declared, 'unless he was inspired.' She marveled at his achievement, considering how 'unlearned and ignorant he was.'"[5] Smith, who never actually let his wife see the plates, hung a blanket across the room to ensure privacy. He dictated what he read to Emma, who wrote everything down.

The work continued slowly until April 1829, when schoolteacher Oliver Cowdery arrived in Harmony. Cowdery had heard about the plates from Smith's parents and presented himself as a scribe—one who could write out the messages that Smith dictated. Now the work went much faster. Smith applied for a copyright

*This illustration shows a passage from the book of Isaiah, written in the mysterious script of Moroni's gold plates.*

in June; typesetting began at a printer in Palmyra in August; and the following March, the publication of the Book of Mormon was announced. According to tradition, after publication of the book, Smith returned the plates to Moroni at the original hiding place in Palmyra, New York.

As Smith translated the plates, the Book of Mormon developed into a religious history of people who had lived in Central America thousands of years before the time of Jesus (whom Smith believed to be the biblical "lost tribes of Israel"). It ends fourteen hundred years before the time of Joseph Smith, in A.D. 421, when Moroni buried the plates in present-day New York.

## The Beginnings of the Church

Even before the Book of Mormon's publication, the first step toward the creation of Joseph Smith's new church began on May 15, 1829. Smith and Cowdery went into the woods to pray. They later reported that a messenger identifying himself as John the Baptist appeared and instructed the two men to baptize and ordain each other into the Priesthood of Aaron. Smith was proclaimed the first elder of the new church. They were authorized to

*John the Baptist ordains Joseph Smith and his scribe Oliver Cowdery into the Priesthood of Aaron.*

induct new members into this church and were given instructions on how the church should be organized. But they were not yet given the power to heal or to work miracles. That power came some days later, when the apostles Peter, James, and John appeared and initiated both men into the Melchizedek priesthood. All those who entered this priesthood would be called elders.

On April 6, 1830, at the home of Smith's friends the Whitmers, in Fayette, New York, the Church of Christ (as it was originally called) was officially proclaimed. "Latter-day Saints" would be added later to the official name of the new church. About thirty people were present at the official meeting—members of the Smith and Whitmer families and close friends from Palmyra. Smith clearly stated that he alone had the authority to speak for the church and that he alone understood its mysteries. He announced to the small group that he was to be called "seer, a translator, a prophet, an apostle of Jesus Christ, an elder of the church through the will of God the Father, and the grace of your Lord Jesus Christ."[6] Smith was also clear that every member of this new religion was to be a missionary who would help spread its gospel.

Word of the new church and the Book of Mormon spread quickly in rural New York. By September the membership had grown to sixty. True to the missionary doctrine, some members began to move out of the region to spread the word. One of the missionaries was Parley Pratt, who went to Kirtland, Ohio, near Cleveland. There he converted preacher Sidney Rigdon, who brought his entire congregation of 127 members into the fold. By 1831 the church had grown to one thousand members. Soon after, Smith had a vision in which Moroni told him to move his church headquarters to Ohio.

Adherents of established religions mocked Smith, his faith, and his followers. Nonbelievers demanded to see the mysterious golden plates that Smith had supposedly translated. They called Smith a fraud, suggesting that he had invented the whole story for monetary gain. When new converts pointed out that the Book of Mormon was too complicated for an uneducated man like Smith to complete, nonbelievers dismissed the text as having been taken mostly from the Bible.

Opposition went beyond mockery, however, and Smith was often physically attacked as he attempted to preach the new doctrine. After the first printing of the Book of Mormon, he was called a false prophet and pursued by mobs. Newspapers demanded that he produce miracles if he was the true prophet.

What particularly stirred resentment among traditional churchgoers was the Mormons' belief in their church's supremacy—the claim that Mormonism represents the true church of God. Orson Pratt, an early church elder, described the Mormon attitude with this catechism:

Q. What does the Lord require of the people of the United States?

A. He requires them to repent of all their sins and embrace the message of salvation, contained in the Book of Mormon, and be baptized into THIS church, and prepare themselves for the coming of the Lord.

Q. What will be the consequence if they do not embrace the Book of Mormon as a divine revelation?

A. They will BE DESTROYED from the land and SENT DOWN TO HELL, like all other generations who have rejected a divine message![7]

## The Move to Ohio

From the beginning Smith had embraced an expansion policy for the Mormon Church. The necessity of a move became urgent in the face of increasing and more violent animosity toward the new religion. As Smith's success in recruiting newcomers grew, the converts' family members complained that somehow the converts had been mesmerized or carried away by some strange deception. This skepticism often turned to anger, and anger turned into violence. Many times Smith's home was surrounded by neighbors, whose threats bordered on physical attack. More than once he was chased

# Historic Kirtland

In May 2003 Gordon B. Hinckley, president of the Mormon Church, was in Kirtland, Ohio, to dedicate historic Kirtland in remembrance of Joseph Smith and the early Mormon pioneers. A chapel, pioneer home, wooden schoolhouse, stocked store, water-powered sawmill, and an inn were all restored in a process that took five years of planning after decades of research. Mormon historians combed through diaries, newspapers, tax records, and historic files. They also examined existing structures to produce authentic replicas. This area is significant to the LDS because it was church headquarters from 1831 to 1837 before Smith moved his people to Nauvoo, Illinois, and then Brigham Young moved them to Salt Lake City.

As recorded by the LDS, Hinckley told the crowd of fifteen hundred viewers attending the opening of the restored buildings: "As I sat in this beautiful chapel in this place sanctified by sacrifice by those who stopped here for a season, I thought of the miracle that came to pass. Those who walked these roads could not have dreamed of the marvelous expansion of this great work."

by angry mobs. At one point he was ordered to appear before the county justice on the charge of disorderly conduct. Smith later said that the charge stemmed from the stir created by his preaching the Book of Mormon. Although Smith was acquitted, he was often back in court on similar charges filed by the townspeople. On some occasions he spent long days in court without being offered food or drink.

In light of these problems, the first westward migration of the Mormon Church began in early 1831. Smith and his wife reached Kirtland, Ohio, around the first of February. Upon his arrival Smith declared himself to be the Prophet to those who had gathered to greet him.

By June most of the early converts had left New York, which would never again be Mormon headquarters. As word spread of Smith's arrival, more converts flocked to Kirtland each month. One of them was a heavyset, striking young man from Vermont named Brigham Young. Converted shortly after reading the Book of Mormon, he expressed joy at shaking the hand of the Prophet. One biographer described the atmosphere as more and more converts arrived:

The pentecostal spirit descended upon Kirtland with the arrival of the first Mormon proselytes. The little hamlet became the stage for a drama of dementia, scenes of debauchery, weird rites, extravagant expressions of religious fervor, miracles, revelations by the wholesale. The news spread like wildfire throughout the Western Reserve, and Mormonism almost overnight became a great issue. [8]

After Smith assumed control of the church in Kirtland he kept adding new offices for the operation, organization, and discipline of the church as the congregation grew. Most of these initiatives, Smith claimed, came from revelations he received—about sixty-five came to him during his years in Ohio, 1831–1837.

But as the Mormon community grew in Kirtland, so did antagonism toward it. The number of announced revelations, Smith's firm authority over his membership, and the increase in converts alarmed the other people of the town. Since the Mormons tended to vote as one voice, their power in the community was seen as a threat to those whose beliefs differed. This hostility intensified when a rumor that Smith was practicing plural marriage spread. He did eventually marry a sixteen-year-old girl who lived in his home while he was in Kirtland.

Once again the growing animosity erupted into violence when a

*An angry mob in Kirtland, Ohio, carries off Joseph Smith to the woods to tar and feather him. Smith and his followers were frequently the victims of mob attacks.*

mob broke into Smith's house and tarred and feathered him. The following morning, despite his pain and wounds, he walked into the meeting hall, which greatly increased his heroic stature among his followers.

This attack was only one of many to follow from people who resented the Mormons' intrusion into their lives and scoffed at Smith's revelations. But the hostility seemed to strengthen rather than fragment the Mormon community, whose members believed that they were following God's direction. God would lead them to what Smith called a new Zion, identified as the earthly abode of God, a place of peace and safety. With divine inspiration, they would raise their families in a promised land.

# chapter two

# Mormon Doctrines

Three books are central to the Mormon religion: the *Doctrine and Covenants*, the Bible, and the Book of Mormon. The *Doctrine and Covenants*, which guides the Mormons' everyday life, was published in 1835 to stop the confusion resulting from Smith's revelations and conflicting directions from church leaders. It is both scriptural revelation and handbook, including instructions for governing the church, conducting missionary work, recording visions, and clarifying the gospel. Over the years other revelations and statements were added. This book is regarded by Mormons as modern scripture equal in value to the Book of Mormon and the Bible.

The *Doctrine and Covenants* is central to Mormon life and church organization. All aspects are covered—from information on how the priesthood is organized to commands to build temples. As organized today, it is a compilation of 138 revelation chapters and two special declarations. By far, the majority of the revelations (133) come from Smith; other revelations include those of Oliver Cowdery, Brigham Young, and John Taylor. The two declarations are the 1890 manifesto on polygamy and the 1978 statement against racial discrimination in the priesthood.

During the period when Smith had most of his revelations, he was intent upon establishing his authority as the church's Prophet. The revelations in the *Doctrine and Covenants* are written as a dialogue between Smith and God.

As Smith taught and as Mormons believe, the Mormon Church diverges from established Christianity because it teaches that God has evolved from man and that men might evolve into gods. Smith believed that Christ came to earth to save humankind, as do other Christian religions (such as Catholicism). While Mormons believe in the Second Coming, when Jesus Christ returns to earth, Smith said that Mormons must make active preparation for Christ's return. Mormons can influence the Second Coming as well. Instead of merely keeping the faith and waiting, Smith taught that Mormons can change the future by spreading good and eliminating evil around the world.

As the main body of the *Doctrine and Covenants* took form, Smith undertook his own translation of the Bible. He believed (as Mormons believe) that while the Bible is a true work of scripture, it had been incorrectly or incompletely translated. In 1843 Smith wrote that many things stated in the Bible did not conform to what had been revealed to him. Smith never completed his work on the Bible. Known as the Joseph Smith

*Joseph Smith reads the Book of Mormon to a group of converts. The book recounts the history of a group of Hebrews that migrated to North America in 600 B.C.*

Translation (JST), the manuscript was not published until 1867 and until recently was the official Bible of the Reorganized Church of the Latter Day Saints (RLDS), a smaller group that traces its origins back to Smith but which broke away from the larger church.

The Mormons use a modified King James Version as the official Bible of the Latter-day Saints (LDS). It differs from the standard version used by other denominations because it incorporates changes that Smith made.

## The Book of Mormon

Along with the Bible, the Latter-day Saints look to the Book of Mormon, officially *The Book of Mormon: An Account Written by the Hand of Mormon upon Plates Taken from the Plates of Nephi,* first published in 1830. The title page lists Joseph Smith, Junior, as author. The book is accepted by Latter-day Saints as holy scripture and is central to their beliefs. Smith preached that this book is a divinely inspired work, revealed to him and translated by him.

The first few copies of the book were sold or given away to family members and friends after they were printed; the initial reaction to the book was not overwhelming. Most regarded it as fiction interlaced with

heresy or perhaps a harmless historical novel. But a few believed it to be what it claimed to be: a true translation of ancient records that had long been sealed and held in the earth until Joseph Smith received the revelation to free the records.

In the Bible, the Old Testament starts with the beginning of the world and contains stories of the lives of biblical figures such as Esther, Daniel, and Jonah. The Book of Mormon is similar in both style and theme. It tells the history of a group of Hebrews who migrated to the present-day Americas about the year 600 B.C., led by the prophet Lehi. Of Lehi's six sons, four (Nephi, Samuel, Jacob, and Joseph) followed the teachings of their father. But sons Laman and Lemuel were jealous of the others, and eventually the family split into two groups. Thus began the great division in the nation. The Lamanites (whom the Mormons believe to be the ancestors of Native Americans) became uncivilized. The industrious and virtuous Nephites developed culturally but were eventually destroyed by the Lamanites about A.D. 400. However, before that occurred Jesus had appeared to teach the Nephites after his ascension.

The Book of Mormon is attributed by Smith to be the work of Mormon, military head of the Nephites from 327 to 385 A.D. From the age of fifteen until his death at age seventy-three, Mormon led his people. The Nephite civilization had seriously declined by this time, and Mormon knew that its people would be in peril until they turned to God. During the last years of his life, he began to write the history of his people.

As Mormon gathered the Nephites together for a large battle with the Lamanites, he sensed that his death was near. He made plans to save the records of his civilization, which he had written down on a series of plates. Mormon hid the plates in a hill called Cumorah and told his son Moroni about what he had done before he entered the battle.

Mormon died in the battle, and Moroni added the story of that last great catastrophe to the Book of Mormon in A.D. 400. Over the next twenty-one years until his death, Moroni devoted his life to Nephite history. He finished transcribing the plates that Mormon had begun, described church practices for the Lamanites, and added two epistles from Mormon. Then he closed the record. According to the LDS, the record stayed hidden until Joseph Smith was instructed to find the plates in 1823. Smith later wrote that he discovered the plates because of

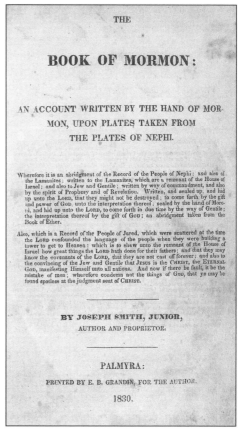

*This photo shows the title page of the first edition of the Book of Mormon.*

"a messenger sent from the presence of God to me, and that his name was Moroni."[9]

Questions have been raised about the Book of Mormon's relationship to the Bible. About one-third of Isaiah is quoted in the Book of Mormon, for instance, but with some unique changes. For these and other reasons, few non-Mormon scholars regard the book as serious ancient literature, a fact that offends many Mormons.

## The Book of Abraham

Another part of Mormon scripture to accompany the Book of Mormon and the Bible is the Book of Abraham. In 1835 Smith is said to have bought Egyptian mummies and ancient strips of papyrus from an Irish immigrant named Michael H.Chandler, who was traveling through Kirtland. Smith claimed to have translated the writing on the papryus strips, saying that they contained the writings of the ancient patriarch Abraham.

Along with the translation of the papryus, Smith introduced the doctrine of a plurality of gods. As he taught the gospel, Smith said that God is one of several gods, distinct from the one God of the Bible. According to Smith, God is not eternal, he is an exalted man, and he is the actual physical father of Christ. Smith later stated: "I wish to declare I have always and in all congregations when I have preached on the subject of the Deity, it has been the plurality

*Angelic-looking men begin a Mormon pageant with a trumpet fanfare. Mormons believe that humans are potential gods and that the church helps them achieve divinity.*

of Gods." [10] Not one god but many gods was declared Mormon doctrine. According to this doctrine, god is a title for many leaders in heaven. A council created the world under God's direction, and its members are called gods. The god of earth once lived in a world such as humans do. And those who prove themselves worthy will return to God's presence and can share that title. However, although both men and women are eligible to enter the celestial kingdom, only the man can progress to god and king and receive all the blessings of Abraham.

Although some Mormons disagreed with this doctrine and many felt that Smith had committed blasphemy, for others it meant that human beings on earth were actually potential gods. The purpose of the church, therefore, was to aid the Mormons in their preparation for elevation to the status of godhood. This is known as the Law of Eternal Progression.

## Baptism of the Dead

To allow those who died before the Book of Mormon was revealed to enter the celestial kingdom, Smith restored an early Christian rite, baptism on behalf of the dead. This rite follows the words of Paul in the New Testament: "Otherwise, what do people mean by being baptized on behalf of the dead? If the dead are not raised at all, why are people baptized on their behalf?" [11] Mormons claim that Paul was arguing against those who did not believe in a future resurrection.

As revealed by Smith, the Hebrew prophet Elijah appeared to him while he was in Kirtland and gave him the authority to ensure that the promises Smith made on earth would be validated in heaven. But it was not until later that Smith talked of this power, for example, when he said that he could restore the long-forgotten ritual of baptism for the dead. This claim seemed reasonable since a person had to be baptized in order to be saved. Smith's followers reasoned that there had to be a way to save those who had died without baptism because they had not heard the gospel.

Smith preached that after death, the spirit of a person goes to a special place to await judgment. In that place, the spirit hears the gospel. Even if he or she accepts this as the true word of God, however, earthly baptism must be administered for salvation to occur. Someone on earth can thus stand in for the deceased and be baptized on his or her behalf.

Mormons believe that baptism for the dead will save those who died without knowledge of the true religion. At the temple baptism ceremony, the person standing for the dead is ritually washed, anointed with oil, and dressed in white temple garments as protection against evil. Teenage boys and girls in white robes often stand in for deceased persons. This is regarded as an honor, similar to that of Catholic youngsters serving at the altar.

Mormons teach that while the baptism ceremony does not "save" the deceased, it does give them a choice in the afterlife. The deceased must still accept the offer to enter the kingdom of Christ.

## Institutions and Organization of the Church

In some ways even the highly organized Catholic Church seems loosely organized in comparison to the tight structure of the Mormon Church. Nearly every adult Mormon male in good standing is assigned a specific church rank, along with corresponding obligations. At the top of this huge organizational structure is the president of the church, believed to have inherited his authority directly from Joseph Smith as the Prophet. The president holds the office for life, and his decisions are accepted as the will of God.

Directly beneath the presidency is the separate Council of Twelve Apostles (the Twelve), organized by Smith in 1835; one of the Twelve is chosen to succeed the president upon his death. The Twelve's decisions may be discussed among themselves and questioned by the president, but not by the rank-and-file members. The Twelve is responsible for running the religious and financial aspects of the church. Also directly beneath the presidency is the Council of Seventy, which has direct responsibility for the church's missionary work. The office of Patriarch was added by Smith in 1833; its purpose is to give advice and special blessings. Smith's father, Joseph Sr., was the first person to hold this position. The practice of patriarchal blessings continues today.

When Smith founded the church in 1830, he established two priesthoods—Aaronic (or Levitical) and Melchizedek. Smith claimed that during the ensuing years, God revealed to him how the priesthoods were to operate. According to Smith, John the Baptist appeared to him and Cowdery as they were praying in a clearing. John the Baptist laid his hands on them and conferred upon them the Priesthood of Aaron. The men were told that the priesthood held the key to the gospel of repentance, baptism by immersion for remission of sins, and ministering angels—beings that can be called upon to watch over the

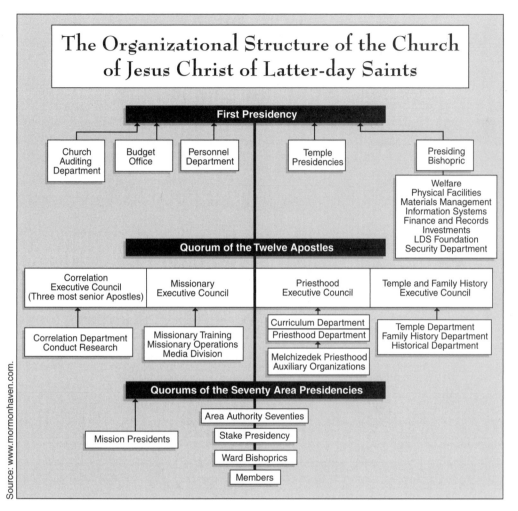

The Organizational Structure of the Church of Jesus Christ of Latter-day Saints

Source: www.mormonhaven.com.

Mormons. Later, Smith reported, both men received the higher priesthood of Melchizedek, which gave them the power to lay on hands—to heal. The men then baptized each other and ordained each other as elders, Smith becoming First Elder and Cowdery Second Elder of the church. Mormons believe that their priesthood is the only valid one in existence, claiming that all other Christian ministries lack authority. Thus Mormons believe only Mormon baptism is accepted by God.

## The Priesthood

All Mormon males in good standing are eligible for priesthood. The priesthoods, which are in charge of the general membership, are organized into various groups called quorums. The Melchizedek priesthood consists of high priests, seventies, and elders.

# The Second Elder

Oliver Cowdery, the itinerant schoolteacher who became Smith's secretary in translating and transcribing the Book of Mormon, figures prominently in the Prophet's life and teachings. As soon as the work was completed, Smith wanted to organize a church, but Cowdery hesitated. He was concerned that Smith was not a minister of the gospel. Soon after, when the two went into the woods one afternoon in May 1829, they reportedly saw John the Baptist and baptized and ordained each other. When the Mormon Church was founded the following year, Cowdery was the Second Elder. Later it was Cowdery who went to Missouri and brought back a glowing report, and Smith moved the church to a site near Independence. However, Cowdery and two others were excommunicated from the church for alleged misbehavior, including counterfeiting in Missouri. He later rejoined the church and was rebaptized by Smith.

*Smith's scribe Oliver Cowdery became the second elder of the Mormon Church.*

When a Mormon male becomes part of this higher priesthood, he is ordained to an office, usually as an elder, as judged by higher ranking members. He may be assigned to duties such as blessing family members and healing the sick. The Aaronic priesthood consists of priests, teachers, and deacons. In this lower priesthood, young men are trained in gospel principles and priesthood duties as they mature. Members can baptize and prepare, bless, and pass the sacrament of the Lord's Supper each Sabbath. The Mormons distribute bread and water (instead of wine) at their Sabbath services in memory of the Last Supper of Jesus.

Eventually, members of the Aaronic priesthood may advance to the Melchizedek priesthood. Advancement depends on worthiness as judged by higher ranking members. Worthiness is measured in terms of personal integrity, chastity, obeying the divine laws of health, and contributing faithfully to the church in the form of tithes. The president of the Mormon Church has total authority over the priesthoods and delegates this authority to others to carry out the work of the church.

If a person is stripped of his priesthood for some reason, he can repent and start over again from the "bottom of the ladder." All persons who enter the church from another religion must start at the lowest rung of deacon. It is very important for Mormon men to become priests in the church because priests are granted the critical duties of healing the sick and baptizing both the living and the dead.

This structure was derived from Smith's numerous revelations dealing with church organization. In 1844 he organized the secret Council of Fifty. This was to be the nucleus for the political kingdom of God, which will be formed to govern the world during Christ's future return to earth. The president of the church (Smith) was also chairman of this council, and nearly all members of the Twelve also served on it. Although this council was supposed to be independent from the rest of the church organization, it never actually separated. However, it did play an important role in organizing the exodus of the Mormons to Utah under Brigham Young. The council met sporadically throughout the nineteenth century and gradually became more of a discussion group than a policy-making body. While its last meeting was held in 1884, some Latter-day Saints anticipate that the council will be reactivated with the return of Christ to earth.

The First Presidency, the Twelve, the Seventy, and the Presiding Bishopric (formed in 1847 to manage church properties) comprise the general authorities of the Mormon Church. This group is also known as the Brethren. Its members are at the highest level of power in the modern Mormon Church.

## The Significance of the Temple

In the Mormon faith, the temple is the place where humans can prepare to become gods. In the early years after he founded the religion, Smith baptized his followers in a river. Then he received a revelation that some rites, such as baptism for the dead, could only be performed in a temple.

Smith began preaching that Mormons could achieve eventual entrance into the heavenly kingdom only through the ceremonies of the temple. That is why building a temple almost immediately upon arriving in a new settlement became so important to him.

Smith preached that the temple is a place where believers of good standing can perform secret rites for the salvation and exaltation of both the living and the dead. They are not churches in the ordinary sense and are not open to the public. Then as now a veil of secrecy surrounds Mormon temple worship. Officially the policy of secrecy is to keep the experience sacred. According to a study, "The temple rituals are the most devoutly protected of all the LDS Church's secrets. Sensitive about the secrecy issue, Mormons frequently repeat the 'sacred not secret' refrain. But official policy is to guard them as secret."[12] A temple is sacred to the believer; visiting one is regarded as a high privilege by a devout Mormon.

The only time that non-Mormons can enter a Mormon temple is before it is dedicated. After the dedication, only Mormons can enter, and even they will be denied entrance if they have not paid their dues, called tithes. Those who do not attend services regularly are also barred from the temples.

In the early years, whenever Mormons settled in a new place, one of their first tasks was to build a temple. Shortly after Smith reached Kirtland, he said that a revelation ordered him to build a temple. And it was to be a fine building of quarried stone and handsomely carved wood. The resulting structure was a large building with a tower that rose more than a hundred feet. It stands today as an excellent example of pioneer workmanship and the skill of a former carpenter and new convert named Brigham Young.

## Polygamy

No issue concerning the Mormon Church has been so despised and ridiculed by its critics as the doctrine and practice of polygamy, or plural marriage. As soon as church leaders advocated the practice for males in the early 1850s, cries against immorality, harems, and female bondage rang out.

Smith is believed to have started the practice about 1835, when he married a sixteen-year-old girl in a secret ceremony. Polygamy became part of his ongoing refinement and embellishment of the new religion. In an early revelation about marriage and family life, he claimed that in addition to a man and woman as well as their children being "sealed" together for eternity, a man could be sealed to more than one wife.

*This photo shows the Mormon temple in Kirtland, Ohio, headquarters of the Mormon Church from 1831 to 1837.*

Since other faiths believed that families might remain together after death, that part of the revelation was not shocking. But polygamy was a return to the Old Testament practice of the patriarchs. That was an altogether different matter to most Mormons in the early nineteenth century.

Smith, who was well aware of the general disdain toward polygamy, claimed that he had received the revelation about plural marriage in 1831 or 1832, but had said nothing about it. Presumably his wife's opposition at the time had also prevented him from further discussion on the subject.

About 1841 Smith publicly revealed his doctrine of plural marriage. The doctrine tested the commitment of many of his close followers, including Brigham Young. Smith told Young and the other elders that they should also marry more than one wife as had the prophets of old.

Historians have given many reasons for Smith's doctrine of polygamy. Some believe that he viewed plural marriage as a social bond against the chaos of the frontier. Some say it was simply his own middle-life crisis, in which plural marriage was an effort to recapture his youth and vitality. Others say that through his translations, Smith had strongly identified himself with the Old Testament patriarchs such as Abraham. The

*Early Mormons practiced polygamy. This photo from the 1870s shows a man with two wives and nine children.*

patriarchal family, in Smith's view, was the very center of Mormonism. Plural marriage was therefore the best way to maintain that authority and to prevent Mormon women from gaining power. Still others believe that because Smith felt his religion represented a new order and was therefore frightening to some, introducing the doctrine of polygamy was meant to test his control over the new Mormons. In other words, the practice of polygamy would demonstrate loyalty to him.

Even at its height, historians say that only about 20 percent of Mormon families were polygamous. Not surprisingly, polygamy was a practice largely confined to the wealthier members. Despite Smith's revelation, sanctioned plural marriage caused many members to leave the church. Disdain for polygamy also led to the formation of the Reorganized Church of Jesus Christ of Latter Day Saints, which separated from the LDS over the issue of polygamy and other practices and is today headquartered in Independence, Missouri.

Officially, the doctrine of polygamy was part of the Mormon religion until October 6, 1890, when Mormon president Wilford Woodruff (1889–1898), himself a practicing polygamist, published an official declaration (called a manifesto), which was added to the *Doctrine and Covenants*. It officially ended polygamy among Mormons.

Woodruff did not declare that Smith's original revelation on the subject was incorrect. Instead, his manifesto stated: "We are not teaching polygamy or plural marriage, nor permitting any person to enter into its practice, and I deny that either forty or any other number of plural marriages have during that period been solemnized in our Temples or in any other place in the Territory." [13]

## The Millennium

From its earliest beginnings, the Mormon Church has been preparing for the millennium—the thousand years mentioned in the Bible during which Christ is to return to earth. In 1835 Smith stated that Christ would reappear in the near future. As their church's official name indicates, the early Mormons believed they were living in the latter days of the world and that they would witness the establishment of Zion (the promised land) in America and the return of Christ. The millennium would see the tribes of Israel gathered at Zion in America as well as in Jerusalem. Except for those two places, Smith said the world would endure great slaughter and destruction; but Jesus Christ would reign on earth for one

*A Mormon couple poses in their emergency shelter. Mormons take practical steps to prepare for the millennium, the thousand-year period during which Christ will reign on earth.*

thousand years. Smith taught that during that time, hundreds of Mormon temples would be built to carry out the ordinances and baptisms for the dead.

## A Clannish People

The doctrines of Joseph Smith set the Latter-day Saints apart from their neighbors and from those of other faiths. Smith's strict organization of the church kept its members busy with internal affairs, except when they were converting others. As the Mormons continued to be ostracized and persecuted for their seemingly strange or mysterious beliefs and practices, they retreated more and more into their own communities.

This sense of clannishness, or insular behavior, still contributes to the resentment that some still feel toward Mormons. The general belief is that if a non-Mormon family moves next-door to a Mormon family, the newcomers will be treated kindly, but they will never be more than casual neighbors. The situation would change only if the new family chooses to convert to Mormonism. Adherence or conversion to the faith is the basic reason for Mormons' existence. In their unique body of doctrine, they believe that they are the only true Christians, as told to them by the Prophet, Joseph Smith.

## chapter | three

# Building the Church

Joseph Smith continued to build and solidify his church despite strife among the converts themselves and growing hostility from others. Targeted more and more with physical attacks and verbal abuse from those who questioned the validity of his preaching, Smith and his Mormon followers found themselves almost constantly on the move. Always Smith was hoping to find his Zion, his promised land.

## The Move to Missouri

Despite the animosity and danger that faced them daily, the small band of Latter-day Saints was growing in number and dedication to their faith. The daily persecution and fear only served to band them closer together. With the unfailing commitment of their prophet and leader, they seemed to grow more sure of their path despite the violence swirling around them.

Yet even the most dedicated leader and faithful believer could not ignore their dangerous situation forever. Smith was especially concerned about settling his church in a safe place before the coming of the millennium, which he was quite certain was near. All the Mormon periodicals at that time constantly emphasized reports of earthquakes, wars, floods, fire, famines, or any other calamity that occurred in the world. The reports implied that these events might signal the chaotic period that would precede the end of the world.

In the summer of 1831 Smith and a small group sought out a new haven in Missouri. He forecast that the spot he chose for his next land of Zion, which was in Jackson County (near present-day Independence), would become one of the great cities of the world. Early in August the new settlers laid the cornerstone for the temple. They also set up a few small businesses, such as a printing shop for Mormon literature. Smith spent the rest of the year preaching in various parts of the country and then returned to Kirtland.

But relations with the non-Mormon communities in both Ohio and Missouri did not go well. In fact, Missouri citizens destroyed the Mormons' printing press. The Mormons received little help or protection from the authorities, who seemed equally determined that they be forced to leave. The persecution became extreme when the governor of Missouri issued an extermination

*An artist's rendering of Joseph Smith preaching to Indians. Mormons believe American native peoples to be descendants of ancient Hebrews.*

order, which directed the state militia to either drive out the Mormons or exterminate them. Finally, in early 1834, with their houses stoned and their haystacks burned, the Mormon community in Missouri had had enough, and members began to flee from Jackson County without receiving compensation for their property. Once again, the Mormons were looking for the promised land.

The Mormons were also having financial problems in Ohio. By 1836, in the midst of a general economic depression, the church had to stop work on the temple because members could no longer contribute money to the project. Smith and the other leaders decided to establish a bank that would lend money to members who wanted to establish new businesses. They organized the Kirtland Safety Society, but the state legislature refused to grant them a charter. In response, they reorganized the venture as the Kirtland Safety Society Anti-Banking Company and issued paper money for local use. The organization went bankrupt, and Smith was charged with violating the state banking laws. While a few of his followers blamed Smith for the collapse of the local economy, most of them remained loyal. Smith led his followers and his family westward to make yet another beginning. When the Mormons

left Kirtland to build a new headquarters, Smith was actually a fugitive from the law for the banking fiasco in Ohio, but he was never apprehended or prosecuted on that charge.

## Moving to Nauvoo

In 1839 Smith picked out a new site in Illinois on a bend of the Mississippi River, about 190 miles north of St. Louis. Its name, Commerce, belied the reality of the spot—six houses surrounded by unattractive swampland in a location that had once been a Native American village. Smith wrote in his diary:

> The place was literally a wilderness. The land was mostly covered with trees and bushes, and much of it was so wet that it was with the utmost difficulty that a footman could get through, and totally impossible for teams. Commerce was unhealthy and few could live there, but believing that it might become healthy by the blessings of Heaven to the Saints, and no more eligible place presenting itself, I considered it wisdom to make an attempt to build up a city.[14]

If Smith wanted isolation and freedom from persecution for the

*The Mormon community of Missouri begins the journey to Commerce, Illinois, after Missouri's governor ordered the militia to expel or exterminate all Mormons.*

Mormons, he had picked the right spot. His new city was practically on the edge of the western frontier. The county seat of Carthage had fewer than three hundred people and no newspaper. Paved streets had not yet reached Springfield, the state capital. The Mississippi River itself was a dangerous area—inhabited by gamblers, bootleggers, moonshiners, and fugitives from justice. The only town of any size in the entire region was Burlington, about thirty miles up the river, in Iowa. Burlington did have a newspaper, however—the *Territorial Gazette*—which proudly proclaimed in 1840 that: "Burlington is the largest, wealthiest, most business doing and most fashionable city on or in the neighborhood of the upper Mississippi. We have three or four churches, a theater, and dancing school in full blast." [15]

The Latter-day Saints arrived at their new home across the Mississippi in the winter of 1839. Most of them had left for Commerce without much planning, and by the time they arrived, food was scarce. The trip had been long and arduous. As the tired and hungry band struggled into Illinois, they became easy victims of malaria in the swampy region. However, their Illinois neighbors, sympathetic because of stories of the persecution the Mormons had received, were friendly and helpful in providing them with food and getting them settled. New people meant more business for shopkeepers and more land sales. Local politicians in the area viewed the Mormons as potential voters. Unfortunately this good-neighbor feeling would last only a few years.

With Smith's remarkable determination and energy, the Mormon community rebounded and was soon ready to start over again. Smith renamed the new Mormon capital *Nauvoo*, a Hebrew word that means "a beautiful place." The name became official in April 1840, when the state legislature issued a charter, and Smith was able to obtain a guarantee of protection against violence from the state.

## Building the City

As new arrivals began streaming in from Missouri and Ohio, a survey marked out streets and plotted the city boundaries. The hardworking Mormons drained the swamps and cleaned out the mosquito-infested

## Child Rearing in Nauvoo

To live as a Mormon has always meant following certain guidelines and commitments, especially in the area of child rearing. As good parents, Mormon men and women have always been expected to bring up good children. The reasoning is that good children will become good Saints.

In the early days of the Nauvoo settlement, Smith issued child-rearing directives that told parents to set examples of virtue, modesty, and good breeding. Children were to be instructed in proper grooming and manners. However, even then, expectations did not always turn out as planned. The *Nauvoo Neighbor* in 1842 complained that some of the young boys were running off together to play instead of being kept at home and that others were engaged in "smoking and idleness." There was also too much interest in worldly habits (such as reading novels) by the young women. Because of these concerns, a Young Gentlemen and Ladies Society was launched in April 1842. It was hoped this would channel waywardness among Mormon youth. Today's Mormon youth are apt to be kept busy with after-school study classes and family home evenings.

areas. As word spread that Nauvoo was becoming a desirable place to live, the religious migration swelled, with immigrants from Canada and Great Britain as well. Nauvoo became a boomtown; farmers plowed the nearby prairies, shops were set up, citizens grew their own vegetables. The census of 1845 counted 11,057 residents.

It was in the city of Nauvoo that the Church of Jesus Christ of Latter-day Saints (LDS) began to establish its own identity as a new religion. The LDS was not a gathering of converts practicing a strange faith; it was a distinct spiritual group with unique beliefs that set it apart from other groups in the community of religions. At Smith's urging, the Quorum of the Twelve took on a larger role in the religious life of the community. They shared the preaching of scriptural commentaries and began to address followers at conferences.

All of this increased participation by Mormon leaders was part of Smith's vision for the city and for the all-important building of the temple. The temple was central to Smith because it was there that the functions of the priesthood would be exercised and instructions from God received. The few years that Smith spent in Nauvoo were especially busy ones for him. He instructed the faithful about many doctrines unique to the LDS, of which he had spoken little or not at all prior to this period. The doctrines included the plurality of the gods; ordinances for the dead; and the endowment, a ceremony that involves washings, anointings, and the giving of sacred names, among other rituals. All of these principles were apparently intended to complete the preparation of adherents for their exaltation into the celestial kingdom.

Smith felt that he had not been able to disclose all the blessings to the faithful at the temple in Kirtland. The most important was celestial marriage, in which husbands and wives are joined for eternity. Interestingly, while Smith did preach the doctrine of polygamy, there is no published information specifically concerning plural marriage. Smith taught other principles connected with temple work during this period. He gave power to the apostles that would enable them to bestow priesthood blessings on the people. In sharing his own power in this way, Smith made sure that the knowledge, doctrines, and directives of the church would be carried on.

## The Right Hand of the Prophet

In July 1841 an increasingly important member of the Twelve, Brigham

Young, returned to Nauvoo after a long and successful mission to England that brought in about eight thousand new converts to Mormonism. In the presence of the other apostles Smith praised Young's great work. In the eyes of most, that recognition elevated the young man to the position of the Prophet's second in command.

Joseph Smith and Brigham Young shared similar backgrounds. Born in Whitingham, Vermont, on June 1, 1801, Young had also grown up in an atmosphere of backwoods revivals, with stories of evil spirits and fear of the devil. His parents, John and Nabby Howe Young, instilled in their eleven children a deep religious belief and a healthy respect for Sunday services. The family moved to Schuyler County, New York, in 1812, where his mother died three years later. After her death, Brigham, who received merely two weeks of formal education, lived with one foster family after another, working for his keep. While near Auburn, New York, in 1823, he met seventeen-year-old Miriam Works, and they married a year later. With the addition of daughter Elizabeth, the Young family moved to Mendon, New York, in 1829, where most of Young's brothers and sisters then lived. Although Young joined the Methodist Episcopal Reform

*Brigham Young, pictured in 1843, grew up in a profoundly religious family.*

Church, he continued to investigate other sects, always searching, he later said, for eternal life.

In 1830 Phineas Young, an older brother, was in Lima, New York,

where he was given the Book of Mormon by a stranger who told him that it was a revelation from God. The stranger was Joseph Smith's brother Samuel. Phineas read the book and despite his initial skepticism, was converted. He later asserted that he took the book home, where it was read and carried about by his brother Brigham, although biographer Stanley Hirshon doubts his claim: "At this time Brigham could barely sign his name, let alone read a complex and detailed work."[16] In whatever way Brigham Young came to know the contents of the Book of Mormon, in April 1832 he was baptized into the church. He also gave up his work as a furniture maker to preach the gospel.

After Young's wife died of consumption that autumn, he and his two daughters moved into the home of a friend. He spent much of the following year spreading the gospel in Canada, but when he returned he persuaded some of his family and friends to migrate to Kirtland, Ohio, to join the community of Mormons led by Joseph Smith.

Brigham Young described his first meeting with Smith in this way:

We went to his [Joseph Smith's] father's house, and learned that he [Joseph] was in the woods, chopping. We immediately repaired to the woods, where we found the Prophet, and two or three of his brothers, chopping and hauling wood. Here my joy was full at the privilege of shaking the hand of the Prophet of God, and received the sure testimony, by the spirit of prophecy, that he was all that any man could believe him to be, as a true Prophet.[17]

After evening prayers on the night of their meeting, one of the men asked Smith what he thought of Brigham Young's sudden reported gift of occasionally being able to speak in tongues, the unintelligible speech of some people caught up in religious spirit believed to be a divine gift. According to Young's journal, even though Smith had not spoken of such a gift before, he answered, "It is of God."[18]

## The Controversial Doctrine

Soon after his return to Nauvoo, Smith told Young about the most controversial doctrine of the religion: a husband should have more than one wife. Smith declared that this practice was supported by the Old Testament and that it was the responsibility of the Latter-day Saints to restore this ancient way.

# The First Wife

Emma Smith is described as a tall, dark woman of serious demeanor and as well educated for the time. She was in love with her husband and not at all in agreement on the idea of plural marriage. They had many arguments over the matter. But Smith knew that he had to win her over to the concept. So, reportedly he told her that the Lord commanded him to have numerous wives. When she still would not agree, he refused to grant her his new endowment ritual. This meant she would not receive heavenly exaltation. Reportedly, Emma finally gave in, and she and Smith were sealed for eternity in a ceremony on May 18, 1843. Emma was apparently given the authority to endorse Smith's plural wives, but according to biographers, she always regretted the action.

Emma Smith remained rebellious to the idea of plural marriage, even using her position as Relief Society president to oppose it until the organization was suspended by her husband. After Smith was killed, Emma stayed in Illlinois. She and Brigham Young parted ways in a dispute over Smith's estate, and her son Joseph III later became president of a branch that broke away from the main church. Neither mother nor son ever admitted that husband and father had practiced polygamy. In fact, according to historians Richard and Joan Ostling, in an interview in 1879 shortly before her death, Emma Smith declared, "He had no other wife but me." She also said, "I know Mormonism to be the truth; and believe the church to have been established by divine direction."

*Joseph Smith's first wife, Emma Hale Smith, condemned the practice of polygamy.*

This declaration, which was a shock to many of Smith's followers, shocked Brigham Young as well. Young had happily remarried after his first wife died. However, although seemingly reluctant to adopt the practice at first, Young took a third wife in 1842. He reportedly married at least fifty-four more times over his lifetime. As has been noted, even though probably no more than 20 percent of the Mormons engaged in plural marriage, the practice fueled non-Mormon communities' anger and opposition toward them.

In August 1841 Smith also announced to the assembled apostles that henceforth they would have responsibility for church business, especially as it related to selling land. At a later session Smith explained the new policy more fully. The apostles were now given the authority to administer all the affairs of the church as the Prophet directed. It is not clear why Smith decided to share authority at this time, although he retained overall power. Perhaps the heavy responsibility of running a growing community was too much for one person, even one as determined and energetic as Smith.

## Trouble Again

As the city of Nauvoo grew and prospered, the hostility of those who feared and hated the Mormons also intensified. However, the community was so financially successful that even non-Mormon settlers began to move there. Although the Mormons made a strong effort to get along with their neighbors, it was soon evident that the two sides had irreconcilable differences. One of the problems was that Nauvoo, through the Mormons' hard work and dedication, had become a self-contained island of prosperity. This success was envied by the poorer surrounding communities. Nauvoo even had its own police corps, the Nauvoo Legion, which was supposedly part of the state militia but was actually under Mormon control. Neighbors resented what they perceived as special favors given to Mormons, and accused Mormons of using their voting power as a group to gain political advantage.

However, as time went on, the Mormons' practice of plural marriage caused the most strife. Not only were the townspeople enraged, but by announcing the practice, Smith had also incurred the antagonism of Protestant ministers, reformers, and politicians. Smith's appeals to the Old Testament patriarchs for justification fell on deaf ears outside, and sometimes inside, the Mormon community. So much outrage over this issue developed that the new Republican Party listed polygamy

Biographers say that Smith began to feel that his life was in danger during this period. He exhibited mood swings of anger, defiance, recklessness, and melancholy. Desperate to save his community from the major assault that he believed was brewing, he sent letters asking for help and protection for his church to both houses of Congress. When the letters brought no response, Smith sent identical letters to the five candidates who were running for the presidency of the United States at the time. He hoped that his plight would induce one of them to take up his cause as a political statement of standing up for justice. The candidates were John C. Calhoun, Henry Clay (who would get the nomination but would lose the election to Democrat James K. Polk), former president Martin Van Buren (1837), Richard M. Johnson, and Henry Cass. Smith's letter read:

*This early photo of Nauvoo, Illinois, shows the Mormon temple on a hill in the background.*

and slavery as the "twin relics of barbarism."[19] When conflict between the two groups became severe, the governor of the state, Thomas Ford, had to travel to Nauvoo on several occasions to investigate reports that the Mormons themselves had attacked other settlers in defense. However, he always found these accusations to be baseless.

Dear Sir:
As we understand, you are a candidate for the Presidency of the United States at the next election; and as the Latter Day Saints (sometimes called Mormons) who now constitute a numerous class in the school politic of this vast republic have been robbed of an immense amount of property

and endured nameless sufferings by the state of Missouri, and from her borders have been driven by force of arms contrary to our national covenants, and as in vain we have sought redress by all constitutional legal and honorable means in her courts, her executive councils, and her legislative halls; and as we have petitioned Congress to take cognizance of our sufferings without effect, we have judged it wisdom to address you this communication and solicit an immediate, specific and candid reply to "what will be your rule of action relative to us as people" should fortune favor your ascension to the chief magistry?[20]

The letter was signed by Joseph Smith on behalf of the Church of Jesus Christ of Latter-day Saints. Only Calhoun and Clay answered the letter, but neither man gave Smith much assurance that he could or would change the situation.

Smith decided that the Mormons must move yet again. An exploration party was sent west to search out a new location late in February 1844. According to Robert Mullen in his book on the Latter-day Saints, Smith also feared for his own safety in Nauvoo: "Joseph Smith, full of premonitions of disaster, actually set forth one night with his brother Hyrum, John Taylor, and Willard Richards for California, but he was persuaded to return the next day by the Mormons who pleaded they would be left without leadership."[21]

## The Assassination

In March 1844 Smith called together Young and other leaders for the purpose of creating a secret council that would be the legislative body of the Mormon church. They created the fifty member Grand Council, or Council of Fifty. In April the council ordained Smith as king, priest, and ruler on earth. This was in accordance with Smith's belief that the governments of the world would eventually be replaced by governments of God. Smith said he intended the council to be a political group that would gain the attention of congressional leaders. However, the Council of Fifty also had highly secret workings, such as investigating and excommunicating Mormons on various charges.

When political appeals did not result in help from the federal government, Smith considered running for the presidency of the United States. He was convinced that if people in the rest of the country learned of the persecution inflicted on the

Mormons, they would respond with sympathy, and the Saints would get the protection they needed. Smith's idea never took root because conflict between the Mormons and people in the surrounding towns continued to flare up. The situation grew worse when the Council of Fifty excommunicated some of Smith's high-ranking church members because of their opposition to plural marriage. After being excommunicated, they set up a rival group in Nauvoo and published their own newspaper, the *Expositor*, which charged Smith with improper actions. In retaliation, Smith destroyed the press and all copies of the newspaper. This outraged the surrounding towns even more. In response to their destruction of the opposition's press, Smith, his brother Hyrum, and two apostles named John Taylor and Willard Richards were charged by the government with inciting a riot and were sent to the Carthage, Illinois, jail on June 25, 1844.

At about five o'clock on the afternoon of June 27, Richards heard a commotion outside the jail. He saw a mob of men with their faces blackened approaching the guards, who merely fired over their heads. The mob quickly found the room where the four men were being held. Dan Jones, a devoted friend of the Prophet, had accompanied the four men to the jail. Jones later wrote that the night before the attack, Smith had calmed his fears by telling him that he was certain Jones would not be harmed if anything went wrong. Jones believed him; he described the incident as Smith's martyrdom:

> The sound of the feet rushing up to our door signified that it was time to beware. We stood by the door to attack the first to open it, and we clearly heard them breathing on the other side. There was tomblike silence for a minute or two, awaiting a shower of bullets perhaps in our midst; and then J. Smith asked bravely and loudly who was there and what did they want? He invited them in as we were ready to receive them. . . . [22]

Jones did escape, as Smith had predicted, and Richards was also unharmed. Taylor was wounded, but Smith and his brother were killed. It is said that as the bullets tore into his body, Smith fell through the jail's window crying, "O Lord, my God." [23] He was thirty-eight years old.

## The Aftermath

Smith's death caused consternation both outside and inside the church.

Many of the townspeople were shocked by the killings, even though they had been against the Mormon population. The story of the assassination spread to cities around the country.

The names of Smith's murderers are not known, but they were apparently townspeople who hated the Mormons. Nine men were indicted for the crime, and a murder trial was held in Carthage a year later. No one was convicted.

However, the city of Nauvoo continued to prosper for some time after Smith's death. Work contin-ued on the temple in an effort to show would-be attackers of the Mormons' resolve. But mobs continued to attack isolated farms, and acts of terrorism increased.

Besides trying to carry on with daily life and to deal with the violence all around them, the Latter-day Saints also had to deal with their own deep grief. Their charismatic leader had been taken from them. Who among the Brethren was capable of carrying on the spiritual and political work of the church? Who was strong enough to heal the deep wound that had resulted from Smith's death? Who

*A member of the mob that murdered Joseph Smith and his brother in the Carthage, Illinois, jail is stopped from mutilating Joseph's body, as his brother's corpse is carried off.*

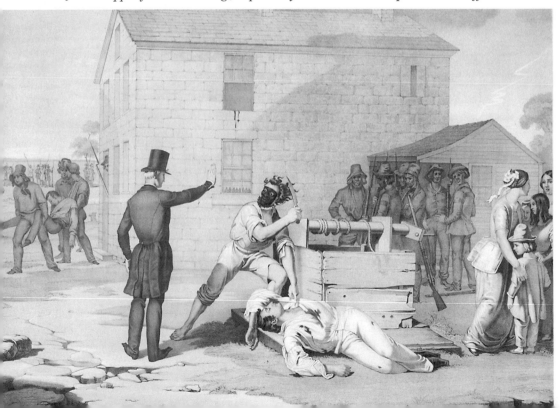

## Dedicating the Nauvoo Temple

In November 2000 LDS president Gordon B. Hinckley and thousands of Mormons gathered at Nauvoo, Illinois, on the Mississippi River for a service that set the cornerstones for a temple to duplicate the original one built there but destroyed many years ago. At this ceremony the president was presented with an American flag from 1841, the year the original temple's cornerstones had been laid. The new cornerstones, which weigh fourteen hundred pounds each, were cut in Idaho and finished in Salt Lake City. With this beginning project, the Mormons are dedicated to duplicating the appearance of the original temple in their historic city of Nauvoo.

could unite the people once again in their search for a sanctuary on earth?

Apostle Brigham Young was preaching in the Boston area when he learned of Smith's assassination. He heard about it on July 9, but it was not until a week later that a letter recounting the death was read to him at a church member's home in Peterboro, New Hampshire. As Young later wrote: "The first thing that I thought of was whether Joseph had taken the keys of the kingdom with him from the earth; . . . Bringing my hand down on my knee, I said the keys of the kingdom are right here with the Church."[24]

Immediately after receiving the tragic news, Young searched out other members of the Twelve in the area. Eight of them traveled by stagecoach, boat, and buggy to reach Nauvoo as soon as possible. Upon reaching Nauvoo, Young was ready to answer questions, calm fears, and reunite the Mormon Church.

# chapter four

# Brigham Young and the Trek to Deseret

After the death of Joseph Smith, Brigham Young led the Mormons westward out of Illinois to find a new promised land. Young was an iron-fisted administrator who contributed little to church doctrine. However, his rules for daily living gave Mormon society a sense of unity in the midst of relative isolation.

## The Chosen One

Young returned to Nauvoo after Smith's death certain of his rightful place as the new leader of the Latter-day Saints. He had been in the service of the Prophet almost from the time of his conversion to Mormonism thirteen years earlier. He had been Smith's most trusted aide and president of the Quorum of Twelve Apostles, the second most important level in the church hierarchy, for more than five years. For these reasons, Young felt that no one would challenge him.

The obvious faith that Smith had in Brigham Young did make him a clear candidate for succession. Yet Young was wrong in expecting that no one would challenge him in his bid as Smith's successor. Sidney Rigdon, who had served as one of the Twelve, the elite of the church, since 1833, was waiting to do so when Young returned to Nauvoo.

A close friend of Joseph Smith, Rigdon had drifted away from the Prophet in recent years because of his opposition to plural marriage. But now he was ready to claim leadership of the church.

Rigdon and other apostles called for a special conference to be held on August 8, 1844. Some historians speculate that Rigdon felt the rest of the church hierarchy could not return in time for the meeting. But the eight travelers, including Brigham Young, reached Nauvoo on August 6.

Rigdon spoke at the conference for ninety minutes claiming that he was the church's ordained spokesman. As noted in Leonard Arrington's biography of Brigham Young, "Rigdon . . . contended that he had received a revelation directing him to serve as a 'guardian of the church.'" [25] This was an indication from Rigdon that he would take care of the church for Smith. The martyred Prophet, Rigdon declared, was still the actual head of the Mormon Church.

When it was Young's turn, he rose from the assembly with these words: "Attention all!" Then, according to daughter Susa Young Gates in her 1930 biography, he calmly asserted that he "did not care who presided over the church, . . . but he would

have to know what the Lord said about it. Joseph had conferred upon the heads of the Twelve, he continued, 'all the keys and powers belonging to the Apostleship, and no man or set of men can get between Joseph and the Twelve in this world or in the world to come.'" [26]

*Brigham Young became leader of the Mormon Church after Joseph Smith's murder.*

The anxiety of the apostles to find a leader, combined with the commanding voice and presence of Brigham Young, led them to react much in the manner of fourteen-year-old Mosiah Hancock, who was in the crowd. Hancock recalled, "Although I was only a boy, I saw the mantle of the Prophet Joseph rest on Brigham Young; and he arose lion-like to the occasion, and led the people forth."[27]

It was a nearly unanimous decision; Brigham Young was selected to lead the church along with the Twelve. Although Young began his leadership as a collaborative venture with the other leaders, he quickly claimed a stronger mandate. Before the year's end, he no longer signed his letters as President of the Quorum of the Twelve, but as President of the Church of Latter-day Saints.

## Young Takes Charge

Young's authority was challenged for a time by Rigdon and others, but he quickly established control over the Mormon community in Nauvoo. That control would be further strengthened when the church moved west. Young oversaw construction of the Nauvoo temple, which was completed at the end of 1845. This also served to strengthen the idea that leadership had passed from Smith to himself. The population of Nauvoo grew to around thirteen thousand as Young called for the establishment of a great Mormon city.

Yet in truth, Young and the other apostles knew that they would eventually have to move because the violence against the Latter-day Saints did not abate. Mobs burned Mormon homes. An anti-Mormon group with the intent of driving the Latter-day Saints from the area was organized. Illinois governor Ford feared a general uprising. Criticism was fueled by newspaper editorials against Young's dictatorial tactics and the practice of plural marriage. Young himself married fifteen women between September 1844 and May 1845. Most infuriating to non-Mormons was the fact that the Nauvoo charter obtained by Smith was still in force. It permitted Nauvoo to operate its own government—including police and a justice department—which was separate from that of the state. That meant in effect that a Mormon accused of a crime would face only a Mormon jury, which outsiders believed meant that no Mormon would ever be convicted of an offense.

As Young was battling the forces of the civil government and the opposition of his neighbors, he was also facing trouble from within. Believers that opposed Young split

*After the Illinois legislature repealed Nauvoo's charter in 1845, the Mormon community was attacked in the Battle of Nauvoo.*

from the church and refused to move west. These groups eventually came together to form the Reorganized Church of Jesus Christ of Latter Day Saints, or RLDS.

The dissidents met to discuss reassembling their church, and what they felt was a "purer" form of the organization developed in Kirtland. Believing that religious leadership had to be assumed by a direct descendant of Joseph Smith's, they asked Joseph Smith III, the Prophet's son, to be their president. He refused at first, but eventually was persuaded to succeed his father as the prophet of the smaller group. According to Roger Thompson in his history of the church:

> The Saints [who went to Utah] . . . were shocked that young Joseph would join a church that rejected the basic teachings of his father simply because that church rejected polygamy. Brigham Young blamed Emma [the Prophet's first wife and mother of Joseph III]. Young Joseph's cousins . . . visited him and tried

# The RLDS

The Reorganized Church of Jesus Christ of Latter Day Saints, or RLDS, follows the original teachings of Joseph Smith, but it is, as described by Roger Thompson in his study of the RLDS, "a church for Mormon dissenters. Many of these dissenters felt that Joseph Smith had been a fallen prophet, although they could not agree on when he fell. . . . The church rejected nearly all the doctrines and practices of Joseph Smith which came to be the hallmark of Mormons. . . . It rejected not just polygamy, but cooperative enterprises sponsored by the church, the Book of Abraham, . . . [and] temple work with baptisms for the dead and endowment ceremonies. It even doubted Joseph Smith's First Vision."

The RLDS, which is headquartered in Independence, Missouri, has followed different and generally more liberal practices than do the Mormons: for instance, they ordain women. The RLDS rejects the teaching of plural gods. It accepts the Bible, the Book of Mormon, and the *Doctrine and Covenants*. Some members feel the Book of Mormon is historically accurate; others feel it is not literal history.

to persuade him to come west where he belonged. When the subject of polygamy came up, they said, "Ask your mother, she knows." When he asked her, she denied again that his father had ever been a polygamist. Joseph politely excused himself from his cousins and stayed with the Reorganization. [28]

Young and the larger group were furious, and for a time there was a great deal of animosity between the two organizations.

## The Journey West

The final blow for the Mormons in Nauvoo came in January 1845, when the Illinois legislature repealed the city's charter. The reason is not known, although it might have been the governor's attempt to restore some measure of peace between Nauvoo and its non-Mormon neighbors. Without the charter the Mormons had no police protection or city government. Even with the Nauvoo Legion providing some protection, it was obvious that the faithful could no longer thrive in this atmosphere. For the church to survive, the Mormons must move away.

Based on earlier studies ordered by Smith, the choices for a new Zion had narrowed to California and the Oregon country, with Texas and Vancouver Island on the Pacific Coast as lesser possibilities. But Young saw drawbacks in each choice, despite the favorable climate and availability of land. California was already attracting large groups of American and Mexican settlers. The United States and England were squabbling over territory in Oregon and on Vancouver Island. There was a dispute brewing with Mexico over boundaries in Texas. Young felt that going into any region that was in turmoil was not a good idea for his troubled church.

In early 1845 the church newspaper, the *Nauvoo Neighbor,* carried articles about the Great Basin of the West, about seven hundred miles east of California. Scout Jim Bridger had described it in 1824. Bridger had gained fame as the West's greatest scout, a fact that influenced Young. Little was known of the

*The Mormons of Nauvoo leave Illinois and cross the ice-encrusted Mississippi in the winter of 1846. Young led his followers to a new Zion in Salt Lake City, Utah.*

practically uninhabited area except that it had once been a great lake (Lake Bonneville), which had shrunk to a salt lake. On a return trip from California, famous western explorer John Charles Frémont had followed the Old Spanish Trail from Monterey, California, to Santa Fe, New Mexico. That led him to the Great Basin and to the Great Salt Lake.

Young studied Frémont's accounts, especially his descriptions of the excellent land and fertile soil. In the summer of 1845, Lansford Hastings, who had also extensively explored the Great Basin, lectured in Nauvoo. He urged Mormon settlement there. Young decided that the future of the Mormon Church was near the desolate Great Salt Lake. Isolation—the nearest white settlements were about a thousand miles away—was what his people needed to survive, he reasoned. They could practice their religion as they wished. And so the harsh westward migration began as once again the Latter-day Saints looked for Zion, this time in the western desert.

## The Terrible Trek

Young led the first group of Mormons westward out of Illinois in February 1846. He had wanted to leave later in the year after making more thorough preparations, but he heard that the federal government was planning to prevent the Mormons' departure. During this period Smith was harassed by both state and federal officials seeking his arrest on charges of treason, collaborating with Native Americans in making ammunition, and counterfeiting. All of these charges were false and were later dropped. There was also a rumor that the governor was sending out federal troops from St. Louis to destroy the Mormons. Young heard that William Smith, brother of the slain Prophet, was trying to get the U.S. president to stop the Mormons from moving west because Smith did not want the Mormons to go west. Young also heard that the federal government might stop them because many feared that the Mormons would get to Oregon and ally with the British there. (The Oregon Territory was being claimed by both Great Britain and the United States at this time.) Whether or not these rumors had any merit, Young did believe that federal troops would be sent. For that reason, the migration—599 wagons and 2,500 settlers—left early. Each family was instructed to have a strong covered wagon and three oxen, plus specified amounts of flour, beans, and other supplies. Even with all the careful preparation, rainy weather and the sheer size of the expedition slowed them down considerably. They did

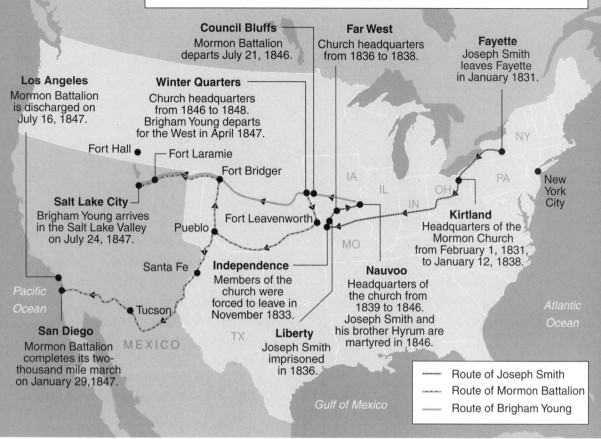

## The Westward Overland Movement of the Church

**Council Bluffs**
Mormon Battalion departs July 21, 1846.

**Far West**
Church headquarters from 1836 to 1838.

**Fayette**
Joseph Smith leaves Fayette in January 1831.

**Los Angeles**
Mormon Battalion is discharged on July 16, 1847.

**Winter Quarters**
Church headquarters from 1846 to 1848. Brigham Young departs for the West in April 1847.

Fort Hall

Fort Laramie

Fort Bridger

NY

**Salt Lake City**
Brigham Young arrives in the Salt Lake Valley on July 24, 1847.

Pueblo

Fort Leavenworth

IA

IL

IN

OH

PA

New York City

**Kirtland**
Headquarters of the Mormon Church from February 1, 1831, to January 12, 1838.

Santa Fe

**Independence**
Members of the church were forced to leave in November 1833.

MO

**Nauvoo**
Headquarters of the church from 1839 to 1846. Joseph Smith and his brother Hyrum are martyred in 1846.

Pacific Ocean

Tucson

**San Diego**
Mormon Battalion completes its two-thousand mile march on January 29, 1847.

MEXICO

TX

**Liberty**
Joseph Smith imprisoned in 1836.

Atlantic Ocean

Gulf of Mexico

- - - - Route of Joseph Smith
- · - · Route of Mormon Battalion
——— Route of Brigham Young

not reach the Missouri River until mid-June.

At this rate Young was concerned that it would take years for them to cross the Rocky Mountains and reach Utah. He decided to send a party of a few hundred single young men ahead and to settle the rest of the group near the Missouri River for the winter. The Mormons camped in a spot they called Winter Quarters, about six miles north of present-day Omaha, Nebraska.

In late June 1846, as the migration was about to move again, President James K. Polk asked for a battalion of Mormon volunteers to go to California to fight in the Mexican-American War. Young decided it was in his people's best interests to comply with the president's request. Not only would it show their loyalty to the government, but it would also provide free transportation west for some of the group. In addition, the money that the government would pay to the volunteers at the end of their year's service could be used to build the new Mormon community.

The group was ready to move again in January 1847, reportedly after Young received a revelation that God had given his approval for the migration. Because the first part of the expedition had shown Young the difficulty of moving such a large group of people, he decided that the entire group could not move together across the prairie and over the mountains. So a small pioneer group that included 143 men and three women set out with the main responsibility of clearing a road into the valley for the wagons. They left in early April.

On April 14 the huge Mormon migration began its historic journey again. It was a slow (sometimes about six miles a day) and dangerous trek.

From Winter Quarters the Mormons traveled through Kearney, Nebraska, to Laramie, Wyoming. Many died of disease on the way. Young himself suffered greatly from fatigue and fever. Sometimes they ran into hostile natives, such as the Pawnee tribe, who demanded tribute to let the Mormons cross their lands. When the Pawnee were not satisfied with the offer of two horses, they set fire to the prairie grass in front of the wagons, but the Mormons escaped unharmed. By May the group had traveled far enough west to see buffalo, and by June 1 they arrived at Fort Laramie. At the fort a fur trader told Young not to stay on the north side of the North Platte River but to

# The Legend of the Locusts

An oft-repeated miracle story concerning the Mormons takes place in their first year of settlement in Utah. A plague of locusts (or grasshoppers) threatened to destroy their entire crop. According to the legend, an army of seagulls was sent by God to eat the locusts and save the crop. Seagulls did appear, but historians say the reason is more scientific. Locusts have a hibernation cycle of seven years. Unfortunately, the early settlers planted in the seventh year and, in addition, planted all their fields together for safety. When the locusts came for their feast, they concentrated in just one spot in the valley. The seagulls went after the locusts for their own feast and saved the crops. It is not unusual to find seagulls in the Salt Lake City area; their fossil remains date back more than two thousand years. Locusts and seagulls still carry on their seven-year dinner party, but now farmers have better protection against them. The next big attack is the year 2008.

cross to the south side and follow the Oregon Trail.

Young took the advice, but the Oregon Trail turned out to be the hardest part of the journey. The trail ran from Independence, Missouri, to the Columbia River region of Oregon. Because it was already crowded with pioneers, there was little grass for the animals and little food for the settlers. Since Young's advance party had not taken that route, they could not have sent word back to the rest of the expedition. The pathway was very rugged. However, after traveling about a hundred miles, they left the North Platte River at present-day Casper, Wyoming. After another hundred miles following the Sweetwater River, they crossed the Continental Divide at South Pass. There, on June 27, they saw the Rocky Mountains. Soon afterward Young chanced to meet Jim Bridger, the first white explorer to see the Great Salt Lake and the man who had helped influence the Mormons' decision to move there. However, Young was not pleased when Bridger said that while the land was rich in minerals, the climate was too cold to grow crops. Yet this news did not change his mind.

## This Is the Place

At Fort Bridger in southwestern Wyoming, site of a trading post Bridger had built in 1843, the Mormons left the Oregon Trail and followed a route into the Salt Lake Valley. Four companies of emigrants heading for California had blazed two different routes into the Salt Lake Valley a year earlier. The route Young chose took the emigrants through the Wasatch Mountains. This path had been used the previous winter by the infamous Donner party, whose ill-fated travelers had found themselves blocked in by snow and had had to resort to cannibalism to survive.

The Mormons' long, terrible journey was nearly at an end when in late July 1847 the first of the huge westward Mormon migration looked down upon the Great Salt Lake Valley. They found messages along the trail left by the advance party directing them on. They had walked nearly a thousand miles. Brigham Young, looking for the first time at the vast stretch of wilderness beauty before him, claimed that this was the place for his people to stay. The main group joined the advance party at the site of what would become their new home: Salt Lake City. Young went back to Winter Quarters to lead the next wave of settlers. After he returned, he never again traveled east of the Rocky Mountains.

Almost immediately the Mormons laid out plans for their city, with the temple in the center of town and wide streets plotted with precision. (They were planned wide enough for an oxcart to turn around.) By the end of 1848 the number of settlers had reached five thousand, and that number more than doubled in two years. As Young had envisioned, the area was nearly totally isolated. A few traders, trappers, and Native Americans passed through, but the Mormons were generally left in peaceful isolation to settle and govern the area themselves. However, the trade that resulted from occasional stops by pioneers on their way to California greatly helped the Mormons survive their first few harsh winters in the Great Basin. They were also aided by the unexpected discovery of gold in California. The discovery sent many prospectors and speculators racing briefly through Salt Lake City on their way to the West Coast. The Mormons gave these so-called Forty-niners fresh livestock and crops in return for clothing and manufactured goods from the East.

But in order to survive those first years, the Mormons had to learn how to overcome drought, frost, irrigation problems, and devastating swarms of locusts. Not only did they survive, but they began to cultivate good harvests of fruits, grains, and vegetables. Jim Bridger had been wrong about growing crops in that climate. Now the

Mormons had made a home in a land that no one else wanted.

## Young's Plan

Aside from his desire to settle his people in a permanent sanctuary, Brigham Young wanted to solidify his own position in the church and to organize the settlement into a political structure that would assure the continued safety of the Mormons. When Young had returned to Salt Lake after leading the second group of emigrants out of Winter Quarters, he called a meeting of church leaders. Although he had been serving as president of the church, he now formalized his position. He reinstituted the First Presidency, which Smith had initially proclaimed. It consisted of Young—who took Smith's title of prophet as well as those of seer and revelator—and his two aides, Heber Kimball and Willard Richards. Despite the unanimous vote, some of the apostles briefly voiced concern that this new arrangement diminished their role in the running of the church. Their concern was largely ignored. This action set the stage for the structure of the modern-day Mormon Church and for all assignments under the Twelve.

Young was firm in his position that he was God's principal spokeperson on earth. According to biographer Leonard J. Arrington: "As for the proper relationship between himself and the rest of the Twelve, Brigham was forthright: 'If this body [the Twelve] is the head of the church and I am the head of the Quorum [then] I am the mouthpiece and you are the belly.'"[29] Young had no intention of informing the Twelve before voicing every basic decision to the people. The church, he reasoned, was not a democracy. Joseph Smith had not tested his revelations in open debate nor would Brigham Young.

As for establishing a political structure, Young drew up a constitution for a government that would even-tually apply for statehood, with him as governor. The state was to be called Deseret, named for the honeybee, a word coined in the Book of Mormon that symbolizes industry. As Young envisioned it, Deseret contained not only present-day Utah but also most of Nevada and Arizona and parts of California and Colorado. (Much of this region had been ceded to the United States by Mexico after the Mexican-American War ended in 1848.)

However, when President Zachary Taylor heard tales of polygamy, which was at the time practiced in secret,

*Wagon trains stop outside Young's Deseret store. Trading with gold prospectors bound for California helped the Mormons survive their first winters in the Great Basin.*

and other stories from Mormon critics, he said he would veto any bill about Mormon statehood. (The much smaller state of Utah was created later.) In 1850 President Millard Fillmore, who was more sympathetic to the Mormons, signed a bill that formed the Utah Territory, and Brigham Young was named the first governor. The territory was named Utah for the Ute tribe because federal officials thought that Deseret sounded too much like "desert" and was therefore unappealing.

Even as Young was supervising the building of the city and solidifying his political base, he did not neglect his duty to spread the Mormon faith. In the same way that missionaries were sent into foreign countries, Young sent settlers all over the West, from Salt Lake City to the Pacific Ocean and to points north and south. Even Las Vegas, Nevada, was originally a Mormon settlement. They moved into the area in 1855, attracted by the artesian springs in the arid valley. But the Mormons abandoned the area two years later, and when the trains came through in 1905, Las Vegas grew into a railroad town. It later became a boomtown when gambling was legalized in 1931. The Mormons founded hundreds of western cities and towns during this growth period.

Young was also interested in stepping up migration from England and other European countries. After the initial effort to recruit foreign members into the church, the number of new converts had slowed. Young decided that the main cause was a lack of money; it was very expensive to cross the ocean and then travel three-quarters of the way across the United States to get to Utah. So he decided that migrants should travel west by handcart (small wagons that could be pulled by a man). Handcarts were cheaper than oxcarts, and the trip could be made in less time. In 1856 about thirteen hundred converts arrived from Liverpool, England, in the spring and reached Salt Lake City by handcart. But then tragedy struck. In August two groups of more than nine hundred men, women, and children left Florence, Nebraska, even though they were warned against starting out so late in the year. They lost thirty head of cattle in a stampede. Rations became scarce, and the snows came early. In ever-increasing numbers, the pioneers grew sick and died. News of the impending tragedy reached Young in Salt Lake City, and he sent provisions. But it was too late; 222 pioneers died, and the Mormons never again sent out a large handcart expedition.

Selected Mormon
Settlements
1846–1899

## The Utah War

As the Mormon presence in Utah grew stronger, so did Young's arrogance and his strict control. Although the Mormons repeatedly applied for statehood, it was repeatedly denied. This was mostly based on Young's unwillingness to surrender any political control to the federal government. As a result the relationship between the church and the government became increasingly tense. The situation

by the mid-1850s is described in *Mormon America:*

Strands of separatism always mingled with patriotism in the Mormon attitude toward the Union, and after territorial status was achieved, relations with federal officials were edgy. When Young's term as provisional governor ended . . . he was not about to move over easily and cede the office to a federal appointee. Through a mixture of Mormon truculence and ineptitude in Washington, a federal governor was not seated until after the "Utah War" of 1857–58, although it was a war in which no shot was fired.[30]

Land ownership and control of the judiciary had long been friction points between Young and the federal government. In general the Mormons made life difficult for any federal judges that President James Buchanan sent into the territory. Then in 1857 a federal associate justice claimed that his life had been threatened by the Mormons in Utah. He charged that the church was intent upon destroying the federal government.

In response President Buchanan decided to replace Young as governor of the territory. He sent twenty-five hundred troops into the Great Basin to establish the U.S. government as supreme authority. In the resulting Utah War, the invading army became bogged down in the Wyoming winter. By the time they reached Salt Lake City, Young, who had heard of their advance, had briefly evacuated the city. The Utah War ended in June 1858, when the Mormons returned to their homes. They were offered a full pardon for their actions as long as they accepted a new territorial governor.

Brigham Young never again held political office, but his word remained law over his people and his church. He was unhappy when Abraham Lincoln entered the White House in 1861 because Lincoln had campaigned against slavery. Young, like many Americans at that time, held racist views. But once the American Civil War began, Young assured the Union of Mormon support. Through the years until his death, he watched with some concern as Mormon isolation slowly eroded from the constant stream of settlers moving into the West. Through all the years of struggle and turmoil, Young remained steadfast in his role as spokesman of God and protector of the Latter-day Saints.

## Statehood Comes

Young also remained adamant about the practice of polygamy, so much so that the issue became an encumbrance to the territory's bid for statehood. After his death, Mormon leaders had to face what most had long known: Utah would never achieve statehood as long as Mormons practiced polygamy. Wilford Woodruff's manifesto in 1890 ended church recognition of plural marriage. Utah became the forty-fifth state of the Union on January 4, 1896.

# chapter | five

# Mormonism Today

The early teachings of Joseph Smith have evolved into a major religion whose members follow strict, uncompromising practices that mark them as uniquely Mormon. These practices mean that every day, members of the Latter-day Saints face the challenge of living according to their faith in a world that often views that faith and its values as outmoded. The ways in which they practice their religion often convey an air of mystery to non-Mormons, which may result in feelings of distrust and even fear.

The term "Mormon" is actually a nickname. Most Mormons prefer to be called Latter-day Saints and refer to themselves as LDS or Saints. Day in and day out they are expected to live up to the ordinances of the Church of Jesus Christ of Latter-day Saints. These are the rules, or spiritual beliefs and practices of Mormonism—such as baptism by immersion in water and repentance for one's sins. It is by living within this framework of ordinances that a Mormon gains entrance and acceptance within the church. And it is only through the Church of Latter-day Saints that Mormons believe they can gain acceptance to the kingdom of God. It is very important for those of the Mormon faith to follow the ordinances of their church because practicing Mormonism will lead them to a godlike state.

## The Endowment Ceremony
A Mormon becomes committed to the core values of the church through the endowment ceremony, which Smith

*A Mormon girl studies the scriptures in a church study room. Mormons dutifully follow each of the ordinances prescribed by their church.*

first performed in 1842. The ceremony includes washings and anointings, secret names, a creation drama, and other symbolic rituals. Typically, a Mormon man receives his endowment ceremony before going on his two-year mission, and a woman, a day or so before her wedding. At that time, they are given secret names for passage into the other world. Although a man is told his future wife's secret and sacred name on their wedding day, she is not given his.

Originally a nine-hour ceremony, the endowment has evolved into a rite of about two hours and is performed once in a lifetime. Mormons are admonished not to recite details of the ceremony to any non-Mormon, which is why nonparticipants know so little about it. Publicly, the Mormon Church describes the modern endowment ceremony as having four parts: First a film (before 1950, a drama with live actors) describes the story of salvation. Believers then go to a room where they learn of God's blessings. Next they move through a curtain that represents passing from life on earth into immortality. Finally they go to the highest level, entrance into the celestial room, where presumably the actual ceremony is performed.

## Marriage, or the Sealing Ceremony

For most Mormons a central feature of daily life is maintaining a strong, committed relationship with one's spouse. The Mormon focus is on the family. Through marriage humans populate the earth by giving birth to those souls waiting to be born. Marriage is not just a holy estate as espoused in other religions but a sacred duty as well to the Mormon. Teenagers take classes to prepare them for marriage. They are taught to abstain from sexual relations outside of marriage and to make sure that the sex education of their children is based on sound moral values.

Maintaining a good marriage means nurturing and caring for one's partner. This generally means that the husband must work outside the home to support his wife and family, although in many Mormon marriages today, both parents work, and the wife must also tend to the home and children. In addition couples are expected to be devout churchgoers and to devote some hours each week to church activities—the number of hours depends on work, home, and financial demands. Mormons also are expected to donate a percentage of their income to the church. They are expected to participate in temple ordinance work, such as baptisms for the dead. And they are expected to plan for the education of their children since most Mormon children go to college.

All these practices and ceremonies prepare Mormons to reside permanently in the kingdom of God. In their study of the church, Robert Gottlieb and Peter Wiley speak of temple sealings, or marriage:

> That permanent role is established through a temple marriage, when a man and woman in good standing in the church can become "sealed" for eternity. The temple marriage is the *sine qua non* for entering the Celestial Kingdom, where the patterns and structures of Mormon daily life get reduplicated for eternity.[31]

In order to be married in the temple, both parties must be members in good standing. They must follow the doctrines and covenants and tithing requirements. The marriage sealing rite takes about five minutes and is conducted by a "sealer." There is no music at the ceremony; rings may be exchanged but are not required. Everything is very carefully planned, and no item is left to chance. Guidelines tell the bride-to-be what to wear, and if her gown is judged to be immodest, she may be

# The Good Image

While most non-Mormons know very little about the Mormon faith, they have usually heard of the great temple in Salt Lake City and of the Tabernacle Choir. Both are seen and heard by thousands of visitors each year. The temple's magnificent organ has twelve thousand pipes and the temple has such extraordinary acoustics that a pin dropped on stage in the midst of a crowd can be clearly heard one hundred and seventy feet in the back. The choir, which is the church's best-known feature and best appreciated public relations tool, first appeared outside Salt Lake City at the Chicago World's Fair in 1893. It was the idea of a choir director, who in 1869 imagined a group of singing voices that were strong enough to complement the size of the tabernacle and its massive organ. Since that time this famous group of roughly 325 voices often travels around the country and throughout the world to perform for thousands of fans. Made up of bankers, barbers, teachers, nurses, and housewives, the choir's members are unpaid and, for the most part, untrained, if one does not count the hundreds and hundreds of hours of practice. They practice every Thursday evening and broadcast on TV and radio either nationwide or worldwide every Sunday morning. The choir constantly receives new members as others drop out; about half the choir at any given time has served less than five years.

*Members of the famed Mormon Tabernacle Choir perform. The choir gives concerts throughout the world.*

given something to put over it during the ceremony. In large temples, such as the one in Salt Lake City, several rooms are used for weddings. The weddings are generally scheduled about fifteen minutes apart. The Salt Lake temple has fourteen such rooms and ten sealers on staff. On a busy day more than a hundred couples may be sealed. After the ceremony the newlyweds usually have their picture taken in front of the temple. All children from the marriage will be automatically sealed.

Converts to the Mormon religion can go through sealing rites as well. Such a ceremony is often connected with the couple's children, bonding them to each other for all eternity. The Mormon Church also has sealing rites for the deceased. Mormons believe that a sealing ceremony in that case may reunite a family that in life has followed different religions.

The strict practices for Mormon marriages conducted in the temple do not guarantee a lasting union. The divorce rate among all Mormons is slightly below that of the national average. The Mormon attitude toward marriage does make divorce difficult. While the church has never actually forbidden divorce, it does stress that it carries eternal significance. Divorced people can apply to have

sealings broken. When children are involved, the matter is more complicated. In a case of divorce, the children remain sealed to both parents, not to one parent only. Difficult cases can be appealed to the president of the church.

## The Role of Women

Long before a man and woman of Mormon faith are married, they have been instructed in their differing roles in their religion. Women are forbidden from entering the priesthood, which provides men with many opportunities. Instead, women are told that their role is to care for their families. The church stresses that both roles are equally important both on Earth and in heaven. The Mormon doctrine "As man is, God once was; as God is, man may become," [32] is often interpreted to mean that only men can become gods. The church explains that a married man and woman form a single unit before God, and that only together can they achieve perfection.

In practical, everyday matters, men wield a great deal of influence. For example, the Relief Society of Women was established by Smith as an independent organization for women and is run by women to aid in all activities of Mormon life. Although the Relief Society continues to do works such as providing good for the sick or promoting education, it is no longer an independent body. Men have the final say in appointments to the Relief Society board, though these decisions are made in close consultation with the Relief Society president. Women are also discouraged, though not forbidden, from serving as local Sunday school presidents.

In many ways the modern LDS woman is told that her most impor-tant activities are homemaking and raising children. For the most part, this mind-set seems to work well in the modern-day Mormon family. However, like other American fam-ilies, many Mormon women find staying at home difficult because of the economic climate, no matter what their preference may be. The church continues to encourage families to have as many children as they can comfortably care for. Yet it is often dif-

# Relief Society of Women

Founded in 1843 in Nauvoo to formalize the educational and charitable work of Mormon women, the Relief Society increased the daily participation of members and brought the church into everyday lives. However, there have been problems between the society and the male hierarchy in the church, and changes have occurred through the years. In 1844 Joseph Smith's wife, Emma, used her position as Relief Society president to oppose polygamy, so Smith suspended the organization, and it stayed suspended for three decades. As though to ward off any further clashes with authority, the financial independence of the Relief Society was ended in 1970. The male priesthood took over all financial matters, and the society was told to stop publishing its own magazine. The male priesthood selects the president of the society. The society president appoints other officers, but the priesthood must approve her selections.

One of the largest and oldest women's organizations in the world, the Relief Society performs good works such as making quilts for refugees in foreign coun-tries and sponsoring speakers such as a family therapist or a counselor on guiding teenagers. Members also serve as home-visiting teachers. Their meetings may offer Mormon women suggestions on career options or good homemaking tips. They serve as teachers and consultants in many fields to Mormon women all over the world.

ficult to care for a large family unless both husband and wife are working outside the home, particularly if they are faithful to the commitment of tithing.

## The Structure of Family Life

Although free to pursue a career, today's Mormon woman is told that there is no higher calling than that of the family. The Mormon attitude toward the place of women in society generally reflects the value they place upon the family. The sound family unit is the center of Mormon life. While there are occasional stories of the young Morman man who skips school and joins a rock band or of the young Morman woman who shuns her religion and leaves her family, by far the greater number stays together.

The typical Mormon family spends a good deal of time together. In the home environment children are encouraged to get school assignments done and to help with the household chores. Everyone is expected to pitch in. The typical family is devout and generous with its time in helping others. The family gives the church a certain percentage of its income. They do not smoke or drink. They are friend-

*Mormon families spend a good deal of time together. Here, a family tends to their garden.*

ly, courteous, well-groomed, and trustworthy. Children attend or plan to attend college. If all this sounds too good to be true, experts say that it is remarkable how closely this description fits the average Mormon family unit.

As noted before, much of the reason for this success is the church's dominant focus on the family. Marriages are sealed for all time and exist forever. Through the family unit, those souls that already exist and are waiting to be born have the opportunity to come to earth. Mormon high school students learn that they can attain the highest status in the celestial heaven through temple marriage. Mormons believe that God is married and lives in an exalted state because of it. This exalted state is achieved only through the family.

Mormons spend their Sundays together, not in the temple but at the local meetinghouse or ward doing the work of the faithful. Children who are eight years old are baptized; babies are blessed, and friends and families of new missionaries speak at the farewell send-off. After a funeral it is customary for the women to serve homemade food in the meetinghouse. Typically, everyone dresses formally for these get-togethers; even the youngest boys wear shirts and ties. Communion is distributed weekly, but water rather than wine is distributed with the bread. Some Sundays are testimony days, when various members speak to the assembled people. They use the *thee* and *thou* pronouns as required and usually give inspirational advice or recount a brief spiritual happening. Whatever is said, the recitation ends with the speaker affirming the true church in the name of Christ. Sunday school lessons, both for adults and children, follow. After Sunday school, the two sexes separate into priesthood and auxiliary meetings.

An important church program that promotes the family is the family home evening. Seemingly in opposition to latchkey children and families grabbing dinner in front of the television or on the run, Mormons are instructed to devote Monday nights to the family. No church activities are scheduled, and temples are locked. The family is expected to spend the evening in wholesome activities, which may include games, sports, and religious instruction. First instituted in 1915, the practice had to be reinforced at various times through the years until it was finally mandated in 1970.

The family home evening is an example of how the Mormon Church controls most private aspects of life. Sometimes that control is not easily accepted; it took years for the family home evening to be mandated. But, in general, devout Mormons accept the church's role in their lives. As a result Mormons are remarkably uniform in their adherence to other church restrictions such as the bans on smoking and the consumption of coffee, tea, and alcohol.

## Education and Work Ethic

The Mormon emphasis on education and work sometimes appears at odds with modern American society, which often values expediency and pleasure.

The Latter-day Saints are very conscious of the value of education. From the early days of the church, Mormons were never concerned that education would cause their young people to stray. According to author Robert Mullen:

> They never let fear that the highest education could corrode the beliefs of their young people limit their efforts, and it is a notable fact that while many young Mormons undoubtedly go through the period normal to all students, where they question and argue and sometimes express doubts, the actual number who fall away from the church is remarkably small. Born and raised as Mormons they usually always remain Mormons, though naturally some are more active in the church than others. [33]

The church is very proud of Brigham Young University (BYU), a 638-acre campus in Provo, Utah, not far from Salt Lake City and founded

*The Mormon Church places a strong emphasis on higher education. Pictured is the campus of Brigham Young University in Provo, Utah.*

in 1875. It is the largest denominational university in the United States, and according to the campus slogan, it is "the Lord's University." Enrollment is more than thirty thousand students, about equally divided between men and women and about 98 percent Mormon (as is the faculty).

About 70 percent of the school's budget comes from church tithes, which makes tuition more affordable than at many other large universities. The BYU school board includes six of the twelve apostles of the LDS.

The rules that BYU students agree to follow illustrate the idea that Mormons accept near-total church control over their personal lives. For example, students' hair length, footwear, and dress styles are church approved. Male students must shave and cannot wear earrings. Female students have to dress modestly, meaning that no clothing can be strapless or above the knee. No one goes without shoes. Everyone salutes the flag each morning and evening.

In addition to their pride in education, the Mormons have a healthy respect for work. Since the earliest days of the church, the Mormons have prided themselves on economic self-sufficiency. At first because of necessity, Mormons banded together to produce crops or to start small businesses to feed and care for themselves. As they became more integrated into society and began to lose the fortress mentality, Mormons worked on achieving the traditional American work ethic.

Most church leaders also pride themselves on being successful businessmen, and their knowledge accounts for a great deal of the church's success in financial and other business matters. In the 1920s the Mormon Church was still located in a relatively rural community, but the focus on financial matters has grown dramatically since the 1950s. Today the LDS is a wealthy and powerful institution.

## The Practice of Tithing

One practice that affects most devout Mormons today and helps to keep the church wealthy is tithing. Derived from an Old English word that means "tenth," tithing dates back to Old Testament times. Tithing means giving a tenth of one's annual income to the church. Tithing was the major source of funding for the construction of many of Europe's magnificent cathedrals.

According to one study, "Tithing and donations are the largest source of income for the [Mormon] Church." The study continues:

Today only about one-third of Mormons pay at least a full tithe

*Mormon parents teach their children about the practice of tithing. Mormons are expected to give a full tithe, or 10 percent of their income, to the church.*

[10 percent of annual income before taxes] to the Church. Their giving nevertheless amounts to a large share of Church revenues because many of them give beyond their tithe share. Such dedicated members believe that if they give more, the Lord will be more generous in return.[34]

Tithing gives a Mormon access to temples and to participation in the holy ordinances of salvation and exaltation. Although Mormons are expected to give a full tithe, failure to do so does not automatically disqualify them from temple access. Circumstances for nonpayment are generally taken into account by church leaders.

Besides this form of sacred taxation, the church also keeps expenses down by maintaining only a small salaried staff and by using volunteers, who are readily available for most jobs. In addition the church apostles, who are mainly businessmen, ensure that the administration of funds is efficient.

The church also has some other ways of making sure the tithe is paid. In 1934 LDS president Heber J. Grant spoke publicly about some BYU staff members who had not paid: "If they haven't enough loyalty to the church to do their duty and pay their tithing, I want it recorded right here and now that I want other teachers there." [35] In more recent years the LDS has tackled the problem of those who are negligent in their tithing requirements by threatening excommunication from the church. Reports from ward bishops bring the offending people to the attention of the church hierarchy.

Gordon B. Hinckley, president of the Mormon Church, explains the practice of tithing in this way: "Our major source of revenue is the ancient law of the tithe. Our people are expected to pay 10 percent of their income to move forward the work of the church. . . . Tithing is not so much a matter of dollars as it is a matter of faith. It becomes a privilege and an opportunity, not a burden." [36]

In addition to tithing the Mormon Church receives an enormous amount of money through donations. Some may come in the form of gifts such as rare jewelry or precious antiques, but most are stocks, bonds, and other securities. BYU, the largest privately owned university in the United States, has brought in hundreds of millions of dollars, most of it from real estate. The church itself has many corporate investments.

Whether through tithing or donations, the wealth of the Mormon Church is massive and impressive. The actual figure is unknown because the LDS avoids public disclosure of its wealth. The hierarchy guards its financial facts in strict secrecy. However, experts estimate its wealth well into the billions of dollars and name it as one of the richest religious organizations in the world. Such wealth often translates into both economic and political power.

## Excommunication

The church, through its president and apostles, has a means of excommunicating members who have proved themselves unworthy by a serious breach of the rules. Excommunication for a Mormon means that he or she is denied the promise of salvation.

The number of Mormons excommunicated each year is difficult to learn. The statistics are kept by an Office of Confidential Records. The reasons for excommunication include adultery (the most common reason), homosexuality, criticizing the church or its leaders, and any type of sexual behavior that does not conform to the narrowly accepted range approved by the church. However, even if excommunication is on the rise (as some report without giving an explanation), it is far outshadowed by the phenomenal growth of the religion worldwide.

## Authoritarian Control and Racial Attitudes

The increasing use of excommunication is an indication that U.S. leadership remains insistent upon being the final authority in the lives of Mormons. Church records on excommunication and other practices have always been difficult for outsiders to obtain, for the LDS exhibits a good deal of censorship and authoritarian control over its members. It does not allow dissent or criticism, which its critics say is not consistent with democratic ideals. However, church leaders declare that their policies come from God and must be obeyed.

In their study of modern-day Mormon leadership, John Heineman and Anson Shupe discuss the authoritarian policy of the church:

The leadership style became more authoritarian as the church increased in size. By 1945 the current practice by which leaders announce a decision and rank-and-file members rubberstamp it had become set. In the June 1945 issue of the *Ward Teacher's Message* (a now defunct publication), the following policy of unquestioning submission was unabashedly defended: "When our leaders speak, *the thinking has been done.* When they propose a plan, it is God's plan. When they point the way, there is no other which is safe. When they give direction it should mark the end of controversy. God works in no other way. To think otherwise, without immediate repentance, may cost one his faith, may destroy his testimony, and leave him a stranger to the Kingdom of God."[37]

Although the Mormon Church is hierarchical and authoritarian, the LDS leadership has demonstrated at least some willingness to revise doctrine in order to keep pace with the attitudes of the wider society.

# A Changing Position

The latest copy of the church *Handbook of Instructions for Bishoprics and Stake Presidencies* has two paragraphs that indicate the church's changed attitude toward birth control and family size. Large families have always been a trademark of the Mormon faith. Now the handbook states that family size is a private matter that should be left to the individual. In the past all birth control methods were condemned by church presidents. In 1987 former church president Ezra Taft Benson told Mormon parents that the number of children should not be curtailed for personal or selfish reasons. But President Gordon B. Hinckley has apparently approved a change in outlook as indicated in the new handbook. This position is more in line with the prevailing attitude of most American couples—that family size is a matter to be decided between husband and wife.

Through the years much has also been written of the church's strict control of its racial policies; however, there is a trend toward greater acceptance of people of color in Mormon doctrine. Its relationship with Native Americans, for example, has been both good and bad through the years, similar to that of the rest of the country. Native Americans have always been considered special in the Mormon religion since they are thought to be descendants of the Lamanites, according to the Book of Mormon. In the early years of the church Native Americans were regarded as little more than savages, (an opinion shared by other religions at the time). But the modern Mormon view focuses more on Native Americans' spiritual heritage. Through the legislative process, Mormon congressmen have been trying to restore traditional Native American lands taken by the federal government. The church has spent a great deal of effort in missionizing tribes in the southwestern United States and has been especially vigorous since the latter half of the twentieth century in fighting racial prejudice against them. Native Americans today, including natives of Central and South America and various Pacific Islands, make up about 30 percent of total LDS membership.

The church has a placement program for Native Americans that is operated by the LDS Relief Society. Native American children are taken from the reservations and sent to school, living with Mormon families for the school year. Many of them are eventually baptized into the church. There has been criticism from Native Americans, however, who resent the intrusion, claiming that in the process of conversion, the Mormons take away Native American traditions and culture.

Mormons have also been criticized concerning their racial theory from the early twentieth century—that the more a person's skin color differed from that of whites, the more inferior the person was. Noted historian B. Cannon Hardy, speaking of a time when the Great Basin area was part of Mexico, said: "Even before the migration to Mexico had begun, Apostle Brigham Young, Jr., had warned members of the Church living in Arizona 'that the blood of Cain was more predominant in these Mexicans than that of Israel.' For this reason he 'condemned the mixing' of Mormons with 'outsiders.'" [38]

Concerning the church's racial policy toward African Americans, change has been slow, but the church did admit African Americans into the priesthood beginning in 1978. This is especially important for African American Mormons, since priesthood in the church is a major accomplishment. Critics ask why such

a policy had been adopted in the first place and why it took so long to correct it. The answer seems to be that the authority for the policy against African Americans began with the early prophets and became part of church scripture. Even with the new official status of African American Mormons, the church's teaching against interracial marriage still holds true. LDS members are admonished not to date or marry a person of another race.

## Genealogy

The Mormon interest in ancestry and race has produced extensive genealogical research (a search for ancestors), which the church began to carry out after the revival of baptism for the dead. Believing that a deceased person can be saved after death by baptism, most Mormons want to discover their ancestors. Baptism will then allow these ancestors to enter the kingdom of God, or celestial heaven, which is exclusively reserved for Mormons. This interest has led to the creation of the most extensive institute of genealogical research in the nation. Its holdings are the equivalent of 7 million books, each three hundred pages long.

The genealogical files where Mormons can find the records of their ancestors and many others are housed in huge vaults that are seven hundred feet underground in Little Cottonwood Canyon, outside of Salt Lake City. The self-contained, temperature- and moisture-controlled vaults, which supposedly can survive an atomic attack, are the main stor-age area for the more than 250 million feet of microfilm that make up the genealogical library of the Mormon Church. It is said to be the world's most extensive recording effort.

Although most research concentrates on members' own families, it has extended far beyond in some

*This genealogical photo album traces a Mormon's forebears. The Mormon Church has the most extensive genealogical archive in the world.*

cases. Searches of deceased U.S. presidents, among others, have been conducted. The name extraction program of the church uses volunteers to submit names of deceased persons from public records for ordinance work. There have been instances of people—known to their families as being Catholic or Jewish—being vicariously baptized as Mormon. That caused some anger and frustration among non-Mormons, and the practice has been discontinued. In the early twentieth century the church's president asserted that no ordinances should be performed on people who had any African American blood. That policy was quietly changed when the National Association for the Advancement of Colored People (NAACP) threatened a lawsuit in 1974.

About twenty-five hundred people use the genealogical system in Salt Lake City each day. In addition, the church has twenty-eight hundred branch centers and went on the Internet in 1999 at www.family search.org.

Whether involved with genealogical research through baptism for the dead or simply volunteering for Relief Society duty, the modern-day Mormon must often balance the demands of work with the demands of family and the church. Businesspeople, no matter how successful, are expected to fulfill their commitments to the church. In the past husbands sometimes left their families for a time to work for the church elsewhere.

Members of the Church of Jesus Christ of Latter-day Saints accept the challenges and the rewards of their religion. Often misunderstood by their neighbors, they continue to live according to the dictates of their faith, secure in their belief that they have found the one true religion and a place in the kingdom of God.

# chapter | six

# Spreading the Word

The accelerating spread of Mormonism throughout the world is largely attributable to the faithful's commitment to missionary work. No job is more important, no message more vital than spreading the word of the Church of Jesus Christ of Latter-day Saints. Joseph Smith himself emphasized its importance at the outset:

> Our missionaries are going forth to different nations. . . . The Standard of Truth has been erected; no unhallowed hand can stop the work from progressing; persecutions may rage, mobs may combine, armies may assemble, calumny may defame, but the truth of God will go forth boldly, nobly, and independent, till it has penetrated every continent, visited every clime, swept every country, and sounded in every ear, till the purposes of God shall be accomplished, and the Great Jehovah shall say the work is done. [39]

The Mormon commitment is to invite everyone to enter their church. To do so, they follow a mandate to proclaim the gospel to all people in all nations of the world. The *Doctrines and Covenants* (84:62) proclaims: "Therefore, go ye into all the world; and unto whatsoever place ye cannot go ye shall send [word], that the testimony may go from you into all the world unto every creature." [40]

In a sense, every Latter-day Saint, whether on a specific mission or not, is a missionary. Years ago church leaders discovered that many non-Mormons either felt threatened by the Saints or were curious about why these people lived as they did. Mormons were encouraged to ask the Golden Questions, such as, "What do you know about the Mormons? Would you like to know more?"[41] The Golden Questions became a church program in the 1960s, and the program is credited with the conversion of hundreds of Americans to the LDS.

The following questions and answers of the Golden Questions program, taken from *Meridian Magazine*, show how questions and replies often help the missionary to interest a nonbeliever. The Mormon may begin the encounter by explaining that the Book of Mormon is the word of God. The non-Mormon may reply, "There are no grounds for accepting the Book of Mormon as the word of God since you don't have

*A Mormon missionary poses in front of the Salt Lake City temple. The Mormon Church has a tradition of successful missionary work in countries throughout the world.*

# Migrations from England

The first Mormon missionary program dates from 1835, when Smith gave twelve men the task of supervising the missionary operations. Although they first operated only in the United States, in 1837 the first English mission was organized. Their first conversions were the so-called Primitive Methodists, who had separated from the main body of the Methodist Church. Within a few months there were almost fifteen hundred conversions. A new group of missionaries returned to England in 1840, resulting in forty-one converts, who migrated to the United States from Liverpool, England, in mid-June. English migrations increased until Smith's assassination, after which they slowed considerably. Brigham Young was also active in recruiting English converts, and by 1869, when the railroad reached the Salt Lake area, many converts arrived from England and elsewhere.

*A group of Mormon converts from England poses for a photo after arriving in the United States in 1840.*

the original plates." The missionary might answer, "Why do you and I accept the Bible as the word of God when we don't have the original manuscripts?" Or, the missionary may speak of the Mormon religion as the true faith. The non-Mormon might say, "My concern is to live a good life. I am against formal or organized religion." The missionary in turn might answer, "Can you speak without using a language, or be taught without knowing one? Can you, then, be religious without expressing it in a particular way. (And how do you know your way is God's way?)"[42]

## History of Missionary Work

Today's missionary work for the LDS had its beginning in 1830, when Joseph Smith's brother Samuel became the first Mormon missionary. He traveled to towns in upstate New York with copies of the newly printed Book of Mormon. By the fall, four of the church leaders, known as the Brethren, had founded the Lamanite mission in Ohio. By the end of the year, Smith could count several hundred members in his new church.

The first mission abroad opened in 1837, when Heber C. Kimball was sent to Great Britain. Thousands of converts joined, and many immigrated to America. By the 1850s missions had opened in Chile, several European countries, South Africa, Hawaii, and the South Pacific, although many of them closed after a few years.

Many of the problems associated with early Mormon missions occurred from the fact that they were simply too successful. The Saints were not the only religious group sending out missionaries to spread their gospel. But because of their immediate success strong resentment of the new religion began to grow. Methodist preachers spread anti-Mormon sentiments on their journeys. Since Mormon missionaries often work in places that have at least some belief in Christianity, clergy from other religions have often accused them of trying to steal converts. The Saints answer these accusations by saying they are merely building on an existing belief in God and are leading the person to the true church.

The Mormons have been very successful in winning converts to their faith in Great Britain. They have been sending missionaries to the British Isles since 1837. A good number of their converts have come from the Church of England, a fact that disturbs its leaders. The assembly of the Church of England once referred to the Saints as "undesirables," and a chaplain summed up their work as the "well-meant but overzealous attempts of overeager Mormon missionaries."[43]

In his book on the Mormons, William Whalen described some Anglican criticism in this way:

> The Anglican bishop of Durham, Dr. Maurice Harland, warned his diocesan conference against "the attraction, especially to young people, of well-equipped Mormon buildings and social activities which alienate them from the Christian faith." He said that the Mormon religion "seems so absurd that we have not taken it seriously" but that "American money and accent and young attractive American men have an undoubted appeal." Mormons have never paid much attention to their clerical critics from the historic Christian churches and they have ignored these Anglican attacks as well.[44]

Missionary work spread rapidly in the twentieth century. David O. McKay of the First Presidency traveled about fifty-six thousand miles for a world survey of the church's mission during 1920 to 1921. He instituted a vigorous missionary program that vastly enlarged the international scope of the church. In 1925 Melvin J. Ballard of the Twelve organized a mission in South America. By the end of the twentieth century converts from Central and South America had become one of the largest segments of the Mormon Church. A language-training institute was opened at Brigham Young University in Provo, Utah, in 1961 to train missionaries for work in Spanish-speaking missions.

## Types of Missions

Two types of Mormon missions carry the missionary effort to all parts of the world: full-time and stake missions. A full-time mission is supervised by a mission president and his wife, who are in charge of up to 250 full-time missionaries. New missions have far fewer missionaries. If a stake (a small local geographical area) is not yet established in a mission, the president has religious responsibility over all church members in his region. If a stake is established, the president performs the duties of helping the missionaries advance in their work. In the nations where the Mormon Church has gained official recognition, full-time missions are established.

Stake missions, supervised by a president and two counselors, are organized to add to the full-time missions in a region. These part-time workers live in their own homes and continue their own family lives. Their work is usually carried out in the evenings and totals about ten hours a week.

The organization of the missions is divided into three categories: foreign; those areas in Canada, Mexico, and the United States where the religion is not strong; and the Rocky Mountain states. Generally the greatest success of the missions has been abroad.

## Who Is Called

Joseph Smith said that a man must be called from God to preach the gospel. In the early days of the church, missionaries were called out individually during church conferences. That practice changed to calling missionaries at general conferences after the church's move to Salt Lake City. That evolved into the practice of sending written calls from the office of the president. "Box B," the return address on these letters, became the symbol for a call to serve at a mission.

## The New York Mission

Not all Mormon missionaries work abroad; in fact, there are many missionaries at work within the United States. Many of them work in the New York mission, which employs about 240 elders and sisters to handle about two dozen languages, including sign language. The mission also has on hand about twenty-five non-American missionaries from China, Russia, Africa, Mexico, and several European countries. Of the four mission districts that cover New York State, the New York North mission extends from the tip of Manhattan up the Hudson River to Saugerties, west through the Catskills, and eastward to parts of suburban Connecticut. The New York mission was established in 1839 in the state where Mormonism was born and has been subdivided many times.

Besides being expensive, life in the New York mission can be terrifying for someone unused to the big city. The newly arrived missionaries receive training on how to become street smart. This covers issues such as bicycle safety and not walking on unlit streets. A telephone chain is set up so that all missionaries are telephoned between 9:30 and 10:30 P.M. to check that they are safely back in their living quarters.

In the early years any Mormon man might be called for a mission. Men often had to leave their families for a few months to as long as a few years. Wives began to go with their husbands on missions during the second half of the nineteenth century. Single women were not called to mission duty until the end of the twentieth century.

The age of participants and duration of mission service have varied throughout the years. Exceptions may be made for special circumstances, such as injury or a problem at home that might delay a young person's mission experience. In general, single men aged nineteen to twenty-five may be called to serve two years. Single women aged twenty-one to thirty-nine may serve eighteen months, twelve months for those aged forty to sixty-nine. Married couples may be called to mission duty for twelve to eighteen months.

## Preparation and Training

Many Mormon youngsters begin their training for missionary work as soon as they can walk and talk. That training continues at the local level in various church and auxiliary organizations. The Priesthood of Aaron, which is designated in the scriptures as the preparatory priesthood, trains young men in the responsibilities of the Melchizedek priesthood, part of which is missionary service. Missionary preparation seminars or classes for young men and women and older couples are often conducted to prepare for full-time mission work.

However, their preparation in theology is limited to Sunday school or high school seminars or theology classes at BYU, and their knowledge of other religions is generally sketchy. So before leaving for their posts, the new missionaries attend a short course in missiology.

Although in theory every young Mormon male is called as a missionary, it is not necessarily so. Before being called for a mission, young men are investigated by their bishop to ascertain if they can support themselves during this period and if their families can get along without them. If they pass on these points, the recommendation goes to the stake president and then to the president of the church. The applicant is interviewed at a quarterly stake conference. When the call comes, it is signed by the president of the church and is a major point in a young Mormon's life. More and more young Mormon women today are called for missionary work, although marriage and assuming the duties of caring for the family still take precedence.

For those who are called, their brief training is conducted at local missionary training centers. If a missionary is going to an assignment where he or she speaks the native language, the time spent at the training center is about three weeks. Those who must learn a new language spend approximately two months in training. Once the missionaries arrive at their assigned destinations, they are given on-the-job training from a designated senior companion and from other leaders. Language lessons continue if necessary.

Course time is filled with lectures and programs. Missionaries live without charge at the training center and purchase meals at the cafeteria, which is operated by the church. Learning the system for addressing a potential convert is a crucial part of the training for a young missionary. The format, which is outlined in an instructional booklet, is memorized by the young missionary and is strictly followed during all house calls.

First, the missionary tries to prove certain points to the potential convert, such as that God had flesh and bones and that Joseph Smith was his true prophet. If the first discussion goes well, the missionary asks the prospect if he or she would attend church at the ward chapel on the

*Planning to reach out to the local deaf community, Mormon missionaries take a class in American Sign Language.*

next Sunday. The missionary also leaves two pamphlets, one covering Smith's revelation about the golden plates and the other an article titled "Which Church Is Right?"

On the second visit, the missionary delves more deeply into Mormon teachings. Then the prospect is asked to read fifty or more pages of the Book of Mormon before the next meeting. The prospect is also asked to start a family prayer time in the household.

During the third visit, if all is going well, the missionary discusses the ban on alcohol, coffee, tea, and tobacco. He or she leaves another pamphlet, which emphasizes these topics. By the time of the fourth visit, the potential convert will have read more than two hundred pages of the Book of Mormon. Now missionary and prospect get into a much deeper discussion of theology as viewed by the Mormons. If all has gone as planned, the prospect will now commit to being baptized into the Church of Jesus Christ of Latter-day Saints.

Specific Church doctrines, such as baptism for the dead, are discussed during visit five. By the time of the sixth and final visit, the convert has read the Book of Mormon, has gone to church at least for one month, and has some familiarity with basic Mormon doctrines. He or she has also been indoctrinated into the necessity of tithing.

The Mormon system is well learned and well presented by the missionary. Departure from the established procedure is not encouraged. Most missionaries see no reason to stray from the path; the system works. And according to records,

*Young Mormon missionaries study on their day off. Missionaries abide by strict rules while serving on a mission.*

most of the converts remain with the church after baptism. The Mormon system and its way of life keep them involved in everyday activities and make them part of a cohesive, dedicated community of people who are working for a life with God.

## On the Job

Missionaries must adhere to strict rules wherever they serve. They are expected to write home once a week, although they are allowed only two phone calls yearly, on Christmas and Mother's Day. If there is an emergency at home resulting in the death of a family member, the missionary cannot return home for the funeral. Visits from family or friends while on assignment are not allowed. Some of these rules are relaxed for older missionaries. Missionaries can sightsee in the countries they serve but must refrain from going to areas that have a bad reputation. They are told that if they cannot correct an evil they see, they must avoid it. They are instructed to wear dark clothes on their rounds, during which they usually walk or ride bicycles. Mormon missionaries seldom drive automobiles.

Contact with the opposite sex while on missionary work is not allowed; no dating, no flirting. The handbook warns against even being alone with anyone of the opposite sex.

Missionaries cannot play football or baseball or hockey, or any rough, contact team sport for that matter. However, they can play softball for exercise. They can see two Broadway shows, if in Manhattan or other city, or two sporting events a year if they obtain permission. They can listen only to appropriate Mormon music, which includes Tabernacle Choir recordings.

The average Mormon missionary is male, about twenty years old, and clean shaven with short hair. Called an elder, he wears a dark suit, a subdued tie, a white shirt, and highly polished shoes. Instructions on how to dress are included in the missionary handbook. Women missionaries, called sisters, are admonished against oversized or sporty clothes and skirts either above the calf or floor-length. This is the image of cleanliness, virtue, and godliness that the Mormons want to portray to the non-Mormon world.

Part of the missionary's day is spent in scripture reading and honing whatever missionary skills are required in a particular area. However, the goal of the missionary is to locate people who are interested in hearing the Mormon message, teaching them the gospel, baptizing them into the church, and guiding them through their membership duties.

Whether on missions at home or abroad, missionaries work in pairs.

On a typical day in a strange city, they walk the streets, politely greeting strangers. As explained in *Mormon America*, the missionary might begin with, "'Hi! How are you doing? I'm from the Church of Jesus Christ of Latter-day Saints. We have a church around the corner. Do you have a minute to talk about something that can bring you happiness?' Responses vary. Some simply shake their heads and walk on. If one is a missionary, one must be well prepared for continual rejection."[45] Without rejection, the missionary begins his or her carefully prepared initiation system.

"Tracting" is what the work of those who travel door-to-door spreading the gospel of the Mormon Church is called. It can be a thankless occupation as well as difficult and draining. While each day is different, it is certain that a large number of people will not be home, will not open the door, or will simply slam it in the elder's or sister's face. Yet these young missionaries rarely become discouraged; they are intent on educating and enlightening people to the Mormon way.

The typical missionary's day begins at 6:00 A.M. with prayers and study and ends at 10:30 P.M. with prayers and study once again. The work of conversion is continual, with one hour off for dinner and one day off a week—called Preparation Day—for laundry and personal chores. Many of the young people use those off-duty hours to serve in soup kitchens and the like. Otherwise they are either out on the streets or knocking on doors to spread the word of the gospel.

For about the first 150 years of missionary work, the Mormons relied on such conversion practices as public meetings, street meetings, fair exhibits, public debates, and going door-to-door with the message of God. Door-to-door visitations are known as tracting, because the missionary usually leaves behind a tract, or explanation of the Mormon Church. Door-to-door missionizing, however, has not turned out to be successful. In fact, according to one study, "One estimate of missionary success from canvassing residential areas was as low as 'only nine doors out of a thousand [opening] to missionaries.'"[46]

Although all these methods may still be used today, missionaries now rely heavily on referrals from other members of the church. This strategy, little known to the public, is called the home mission program. According to Heineman and Shupe in their study, the Mormon Church "swelled from 2,614,340 members to 4,180,000 between 1967 and 1977 and its home mission program helps explain why. Sociologists Rodney

# The Supreme Court Rules on Door to Door

Tracting is the business of going from door to door unannounced to deliver a message. The message may be "buy my encyclopedia" or "vote for this candidate" or "let me tell you why you should join this religion." For many people it is a way to make a living. For others such as Mormons it is one of the ways to spread the word of their gospel.

Anyone who spends time knocking unannounced on front doors across the nation is sure to encounter a range of responses. Missionaries, who spend their waking hours in this activity on assignment, are likely to encounter rudeness and rejection as well as acceptance and kindness. But many people, whether or not they are rude, are opposed to so-called tracting, and they finally took the matter to the Supreme Court. Those who find tracting an annoyance wanted to ban people from such activities. But on June 18, 2002, the Supreme Court ruled that local government cannot demand permits from missionaries or anyone else who wants to solicit items or ideas from visiting people door-to-door. The Court said that those who wish to spread religious ideas do not have to stop and ask the government's permission before doing so. Tracting may not be the easiest way to get one's message across, but it is legal.

Stark and William Sims Bainbridge recently analyzed the subtle strategy of the home mission program in these terms:

> [Door-to-door] missionaries do not serve as the primary instrument of recruitment to the Mormon faith. Instead, recruitment is accomplished primarily by the rank and file of the church as they construct intimate interpersonal ties with non-Mormons and thus link them in a Mormon social network. [47]

## Targeting Specific Groups

Although the Mormons have a mission to convert people worldwide, they also focus on specific groups. Beginning in the 1970s, they wanted to open Communist nations to their missionaries, often using performing troups from Brigham Young University as cultural ambassadors. Touring groups from BYU have performed in Poland, and the university's American folk dancers toured a number of Communist bloc countries in the late twentieth century. In 1983 the LDS was given permission to break ground for a temple in Frei-berg, in what was then East Germany. The idea is to present a wholesome and attractive face to people who have not heard good things about America and religion and to interest others in the faith of the Latter-day Saints.

Still in its early stages but very impressive is the growing Mormon influence in mainland China. Begin-ning with a visit to Salt Lake City in 1981 by China's ambassador to the United States, relations have improved to the point where Mormon tours have been allowed on the Chinese main-land. Some leaders feel that China holds great potential for the Mormon Church because there are so many Chinese who may be possible converts.

## Success Stories

With more than 11 million members worldwide and growing at a rapid rate, the Mormon Church can point with satisfaction to its successful mission-ary program. One example of success is the missionary achievements in the kingdom of Tonga, a small island country in Polynesia. LDS leaders have frequently predicted that Tonga will become the first Mormon coun-try in the world. Missionary work has been going on there for more than a century.

The first missionaries arrived in Tonga in 1891. After six years, they had added only six converts and the mission was closed. In 1907 the mis-sionaries tried again. For some reason

*Mormon missionaries in Harlem, New York, teach a woman about their faith. Most converts who are baptized into the church remain lifelong members.*

they were more successful in getting their message across, and an independent Tongan mission was established in 1916. By 1920 the Mormons could count about a thousand members in Tonga.

A good example of why the Mormons are so successful in missionary work can be found in the Hamiltons of Agoura Hills, Utah. They are the dedicated people who believe it is not just their duty but their happy obligation to serve. The church relies on such people to spread its message.

In 2003 the Hamiltons readied themselves to leave their home, where they had lived for nineteen years, to spend three years in the Belgium/Netherlands mission. Kevin Hamilton resigned from his job as CEO of a telecommunications company and, with his wife and four of their six children, began to serve their church abroad. The Hamiltons rented out their home in Utah and stayed at a house provided by the church. However, most living expenses are theirs, and they will receive no salary for the three years.

Son Matt, eighteen when the family left, stayed in Brussels for only a

*These Guatemalan women are among the millions of people worldwide who have converted to Mormonism.*

few months and then went on his own mission. The younger children all looked forward to the experience. Of the two Hamilton children left behind, Ryan attends Utah Valley State College and Michele, who is married, is expecting her first child.

While on assignment, all the Hamiltons study both French and Dutch. All of them feel that they are fortunate to have an opportunity to serve their faith. Says Kevin, "We have been given so much. We are pleased to be able to give something back for a few years."[48]

# The Mormon Message: In This World and of This World

The Mormon Church, authoritarian and secretive in structure, exists in a democratic, open American society and continues to draw converts as it spreads its messsage of comfort, peace, and strength. The Mormon message is assurance: the Mormon is the child of God and a member of the one true religion. The message is also a crusade. Mormons have been designated through the first Prophet, Joseph Smith, to bring their religious philosophy to the world.

It is this sense of superiority in the world of religion, of not merely coexisting with other faiths but overtaking them that so often brings down the wrath of others upon Mormon heads. Yet despite verbal and physical persecution through the years, the Church of Jesus Christ of Latter-day Saints continues to grow at an amazing rate.

Mormonism is a uniquely American religion. For believers the biblical Garden of Eden was actually located around the area of present-day Independence, Missouri, to which the Lord will one day return. Church headquarters are on

*Mormons march in a Columbus Day parade in New York City. Mormons pride themselves on their patriotism and their contributions to American society.*

U.S. soil, and the church itself is governed exclusively by Americans.

And Mormons place great value on their Americanism. They are dedicated, patriotic, and hard-working Americans who show their willingness to engage in the political process to further the interests of the LDS. They believe they are the people chosen by God in the New World. They are deeply concerned about how their faith is seen by outsiders. They place great value on the family, which provides an island of stability in what often seems to be a world in turmoil. Long viewed as a model minority, they are increasingly making their presence felt as they travel through this world while preparing to live forever in the next.

# Notes

## Chapter 1: Joseph Smith and the Origins of Mormonism

1. Richard L. Bushman, *Joseph Smith and the Beginnings of Mormonism.* Chicago: University of Illinois Press, 1984, p. 54.
2. Quoted in William Mulder and A. Russell Mortensen, eds., *Among the Mormons.* New York: Knopf, 1958, pp. 11–12.
3. Quoted in Bushman, *Joseph Smith,* p. 61.
4. Quoted in Robert V. Remini, *Joseph Smith.* New York: Viking, 2002, p. 57.
5. Quoted in Remini, *Joseph Smith,* p. 57.
6. Quoted in Robert Gottlieb and Peter Wiley, *America's Saints: The Rise of Mormon Power.* New York: Putnam, 1984, p. 36.
7. Quoted in John Heineman and Anson Shupe, *The Mormon Corporate Empire.* Boston: Beacon, 1985, p. 105.
8. Harry M. Beardsley, *Joseph Smith and His Mormon Empire.* Boston: Houghton Mifflin, 1931, p. 105.

## Chapter 2: Mormon Doctrines

9. Quoted in Bushman, *Joseph Smith,* p. 119.
10. Quoted in William J. Whalen, *The Latter-day Saints in the Modern Day World.* New York: John Day, 1964, p. 89.
11. 1 Cor. 15.29. Revised Standard Version.
12. Heineman and Shupe, *Mormon Corporate Empire,* p. 192.
13. Quoted in Richard N. Ostling and Joan K. Ostling, *Mormon America: The Power and the Promise.* New York: HarperCollins, 1999, p. 72.

## Chapter 3: Building the Church

14. Quoted in Beardsley, *Joseph Smith,* p. 195.
15. Quoted in Beardsley, *Joseph Smith,* p. 198.
16. Stanley P. Hirshon, *The Lion of the Lord: A Biography of Brigham Young.* New York: Knopf, 1969, p. 9.
17. Quoted in Leonard J. Arrington, *Brigham Young: American Moses.* New York: Knopf, 1985, p. 34.
18. Quoted in Arrington, *Brigham Young,* p. 34.
19. Quoted in Claudia Lauper Bushman and Richard Lyman Bushman, *Mormons in America.* New York: Oxford University Press, 1999, p. 89.
20. Quoted in Beardsley, *Joseph Smith,* p. 308–309.
21. Robert Mullen, *The Latter-day Saints: The Mormons Yesterday and Today.* New York: Doubleday, 1966, p. 79.
22. Dan Jones, "The Martyrdom of Joseph Smith and His Brother Hyrum," *BYU Studies,* vol. 24, Winter 1984, p. 89.
23. Quoted in Mullen, *Latter-day Saints,* p. 82.
24. Quoted in Arrington, *Brigham Young,* p. 111.

## Chapter 4: Brigham Young and the Trek to Deseret

25. Arrington, *Brigham Young*, p. 113.
26. Susa Young Gates, *The Life Story of Brigham Young*. Freeport, NY: Books for Libraries Press, 1971, pp. 44–45.
27. Quoted in Arrington, *Brigham Young*, p. 115.
28. Thompson, *Mormon Church*, p. 149.
29. Arrington, *Brigham Young*, p. 155.
30. Ostling and Ostling, *Mormon America*, p. 53.

## Chapter 5: Mormonism Today

31. Robert Gottlieb and Peter Wiley, *America's Saints: The Rise of Mormon Power*. New York: Putnam, 1984, p. 189.
32. Gottlieb and Wiley, p. 189.
33. Mullen, *Latter-day Saints*, pp. 229–30.
34. Heineman and Shupe, *Mormon Corporate Empire*, p. 102.
35. Quoted in Heineman and Shupe, *Mormon Corporate Empire*, p. 103.
36. Quoted in Church of Jesus Christ of Latter-day Saints, "Frequently Asked Questions." www.mormon.org.
37. Heineman and Shupe, *Mormon Corporate Empire*, p. 197.
38. Quoted in Heineman and Shupe, *Mormon Corporate Empire*, p. 223.

## Chapter 6: Spreading the Word

39. Quoted in Dean B. Cleverly, "Missions," June 2, 2003. www.lightplanet.com.
40. Quoted in Cleverly, "Missions."
41. Quoted in Thompson, *The Mormon Church*, p. 193.
42. Truman G. Madsen "11 Golden Questions for Brassy Objections," *Meridian Magazine*. www.meridianmagazine.com.
43. Quoted in Whalen, *Latter-day Saints*, p. 232.
44. Whalen, *Latter-day Saints*, p. 232.
45. Quoted in Heineman and Shupe, *Mormon Corporate Empire*, p. 31.
46. Quoted in Heineman and Shupe, *Mormon Corporate Empire*, p. 30.
47. Quoted in Heineman and Shupe, *Mormon Corporate Empire*, p. 31.
48. Julia Rogers, "Family Embarking on Church Mission Abroad," *Ventura County Star*, June 2, 2003. www.insidevc.com.

# For Further Reading

## Books

Carol Rust Nash, *The Mormon Trail and the Latter Day Saints in American History.* Berkeley Heights, NJ: Enslow, 1999. This book gives an excellent account of Brigham Young's leading the Mormon migration to Utah.

Richard N. Ostling and Joan K. Ostling, *Mormon America: The Power and the Promise.* New York: HarperCollins, 1999. An informative, easy-to-read introduction to the practices and doctrines of Mormonism.

Robert V. Remini, *Joseph Smith.* New York: Viking, 2002. An in-depth biography of the prophet whose determination led to the growth and power of one of the world's fastest growing religions.

Roger Thompson, *The Mormon Church.* New York: Hippocrene, 1993. From the earliest revelations to the might and power of the modern church, the author outlines the beliefs and workings of the Mormon Church in America.

Jean Kinney Williams, *The Mormons.* New York: Watts, 1996. This book recounts the history of the Latter-day Saints from their beginnings in New York to modern times.

## Websites

**The Church of Jesus Christ of Latter Day Saints Information Site** (www.mormon.org). This website offers information about Mormon doctrine and practices for those interested in the religion.

**The Official Internet Site of the Church of Jesus Christ of Latter Day Saints** (www.lds.org). The official website of the Mormon Church offers a history of the church, a guide to Mormon historic sites, church newsletters, plus links to genealogical resources.

# Works Consulted

## Books

Leonard J. Arrington, *Brigham Young: American Moses*. New York: Knopf, 1985. A book that places the Mormon leader in historical perspective, using personal diaries, documents, and letters.

Will Bagley, *Blood of the Prophets: Brigham Young and the Massacre at Mountain Meadows*. Norman: University of Oklahoma Press, 2002. The involvement of territorial governor Brigham Young in the 1857 massacre that took place during the so-called Utah War, a disagreement between the Mormons and the federal government.

Harry M. Beardsley, *Joseph Smith and His Mormon Empire*. Boston: Houghton Mifflin, 1931. Traces the beginnings of the Mormon Church from Smith's revelations in New York State to his assassination in Illinois.

Claudia Lauper Bushman and Richard Lyman Bushman, *Mormons in America*. New York: Oxford University Press, 1999. The authors discuss the place of the Mormon Church in America, detailing its religious and political growth from the early beginnings to modern times.

Richard L. Bushman, *Joseph Smith and the Beginnings of Mormonism*. Chicago: University of Illinois Press, 1984. The early years of the leader, detailing the circumstances of his revelations that led to the founding of the Mormon Church.

Susa Young Gates, *The Life Story of Brigham Young*. Freeport, NY: Books for Libraries Press, 1971. A reprint of the 1930 biography by one of his daughters detailing the life of Brigham Young, whom she credits with building an empire in the "uncharted wastes of Western America."

Robert Gottlieb and Peter Wiley, *America's Saints: The Rise of Mormon Power*. New York: Putnam, 1984. The focus is on the importance of business and politics in the organization and growth of the Mormon Church.

John Heineman and Anson Shupe, *The Mormon Corporate Empire*. Boston: Beacon, 1985. How business holdings and political know-how have contributed to the wealth and power of the Mormon Church.

Stanley P. Hirshon, *The Lion of the Lord: A Biography of Brigham Young*. New York: Knopf, 1969. A full-scale biography of a charismatic leader who rose to become the second Prophet of the Mormon Church.

William Mulder and A. Russell Mortensen, eds., *Among the Mormons*. New York: Knopf, 1958. A study of what it means to follow the dictates and practices of the Mormon Church.

Robert Mullen, *The Latter-day Saints: The Mormons Today and Yesterday*. New York: Doubleday, 1966. The growth of the Mormon Church from its beginnings in northern New York to its growth as a major religion.

Jan Shipps, *Mormonism: The Story of a New Religious Tradition.* Urbana: University of Illinois Press, 1985. A comprehensive look at a major religion that is little known to most Americans.

Irving Wallace, *The Twenty-seventh Wife.* New York: Simon & Schuster, 1961. The story of Brigham Young's last wife and her fight against the American harem.

William J. Whalen, *The Latter-day Saints in the Modern Day World.* New York: John Day, 1964. Using historical background, the author places the present-day (of the 1960s) Latter-day Saints in the modern world.

Kenneth H. Winn, *Exiles in a Land of Liberty: Mormons in America, 1830–1846.* Chapel Hill: University of North Carolina Press, 1989. A reinterpretation of the early history of the Mormon Church.

## Periodical

Dan Jones, "The Martyrdom of Joseph Smith and His Brother Hyrum," *BYU Studies,* vol. 24, Winter 1984.

## Internet Sources

"The Church of Jesus Christ of Latter-day Saints," June 8, 2003, www.mormon.org.

Dean B. Cleverly, "Missions," www.lightplanet.com.

John Elvin, "The Madness at Mountain Meadows," *Insight,* proxy2.library.uicu.edu.

Thurman G. Madsen "11 Golden Questions for Brassy Objections," *Meridian Magazine,* www.meridianmagazine.com.

Julia Rogers, "Family Embarking on Church Mission Abroad," *Ventura County Star,* June 2, 2003. www.insidevc.com.

# Index

Aaronic priesthood, 17, 28–29, 30–31
African Americans, 66, 81, 83
apostles, 17, 42, 62
Arrington, Leonard J., 53, 62–63

Bainbridge, William Sims, 95
Ballard, Melvin J., 88
baptism
    of children, 74
    for the dead, 6, 27–28, 81, 83
    of Smith and Cowdery, 29, 30
    temple and, 31
Bible
    polygamy in, 33, 34
    similarities of Book of Mormon to, 24, 25
    translated by Smith, 23–24
    versions of, used, 24
*Biographical Sketches of Joseph Smith, the Prophet, and His Progenitors for Many Generations* (Lucy Mack Smith), 13
birth control, 80
Book of Abraham, 26
Book of Mormon
    contents of, 14, 17, 24, 25
    full title of, 24
    importance of, 6, 24
    Moroni and, 14–15, 25

non-Mormon reaction to, 18
published, 17
RLDS and, 56
translated, 14, 15–16
Box B letters, 89
Brethren, 31, 87
Bridger, Jim, 57, 61
Brigham Young University (BYU), 75–76, 78, 88, 95
Buchanan, James, 66
Bushman, Richard L., 12

Calhoun, John C., 48
callings, 89–90
celestial marriage, 42
child rearing, 41, 69
China, 96
Christians, traditional
    beliefs of, 22–23
    membership growth and, 37
    opinion of, about Book of Mormon, 18
    Mormons today, 36
    move to Kirtland, 19–21
    Joseph Smith, 18, 19–20
Church of Christ. *See* Church of Jesus Christ of Latter-day Saints
Church of England, 87–88
Church of Jesus Christ of Latter-day Saints (LDS)

assassination of Joseph Smith and, 50–54
authoritarian nature of, 74, 76, 79
development of, 42
finances of, 8, 76–78
modern leadership of, 79
official Bible of, 24
officially proclaimed as, 18
organization of
    *Doctrine and Covenants* and, 22
    Joseph Smith and, 20, 28–31
    Young and, 62–63
preferred terms for members of, 67
Sunday services of, 74
*see also* Mormonism
Civil War, 66
Clay, Henry, 48
Commerce, Illinois, 39–41
Communist nations, 95–96
Council of Fifty, 31, 48, 49
Council of Seventy, 28, 31
Council of Twelve Apostles (the Twelve)
    importance of, 31, 42, 52
    responsibilities of, 28
    Young and, 63
Cowdery, Oliver, 30
    *Doctrine and Covenants* and, 22

position of, 29
revelation of, 17
translation of Book of
    Mormon and, 16
Cumorah, 25

Deseret, 63
dissent, 79
divination, 10
divorce, 71
*Doctrine and Covenants*,
    22
    on missionary work, 84
    polygamy in, 35
    RLDS and, 56
door-to-door missionizing,
    94, 95

East Germany, 96
education, 75–76, 78, 88,
    95
elders, 17, 29
Elijah, 27
endowment ceremony, 42,
    45, 67–68
England, 86, 87–88
European immigrants, 64
excommunication, 30, 48,
    49, 78–79
*Expositor* (newspaper), 49

families
    child-rearing, 41, 69
    daily life of, 73–74
    importance of, 69, 73
    missionary work by, 97
    patriarchal authority in,
        35
    reunification after
        death of, 6
    sealing ceremony and,
        71

size of, 80
strains on, 72–73
*see also* marriage(s)
First Presidency, 28, 31,
    62
First Vision, 12–13
Ford, Thomas, 47, 54
Frémont, John Charles,
    58
full-time missions, 88

Garden of Eden, 98
Gates, Susa Young, 53
genealogy, 81–83
gods, plurality of, 26–27,
    56
Golden Questions, 85, 87
Gottlieb, Robert, 69
Grand Council. *See*
    Council of Fifty
Grant, J. Heber, 78
Great Awakening, 10
Great Basin, 57–58
Great Britain, 86, 87–88

Hale, Emma. *See* Smith,
    Emma Hale
Hamilton, Kevin, 97
Hamilton, Matt, 97
Hamilton, Michele, 97
Hamilton, Ryan, 97
Hancock, Mosiah, 54
*Handbook of Instructions
    for Bishoprics and Stake
    Presidencies*, 80
handcarts, 64
Hardy, B. Cannon, 81
Harland, Maurice, 88
Harmony, Pennsylvania,
    15, 16
Hastings, Lansford, 58

Heineman, John, 79, 94
Hinckley, Gordon B.
    family size and, 80
    Historic Kirtland and,
        19
    Nauvoo temple and, 51
    on tithing, 78
Hirshon, Stanley, 44
Hispanics, 81
Historic Kirtland, 19
home mission program,
    94–95

Independence, Missouri,
    35, 56, 98

Jackson County, Missouri,
    38–39
Jesus Christ
    beliefs about, 6
    millennium and, 23,
        35–36, 37–38
    Nephites and, 24
John the Baptist, 17, 28,
    30
Joseph Smith Translation
    (JST) of Bible, 23–24

Kimball, Heber C., 62, 87
Kirtland, Ohio
    financial problems in,
        39
    missionary work in, 18
    move to, 19–21
    temple in, 32, 39

Lamanite Mission, 87
Lamanites, 24, 25, 80
Law of Eternal
    Progression, 27
Lehi, 24

Levitical priesthood. *See*
Aaronic priesthood
locusts, legend of, 60

marriage(s)
celestial, 42
divorce and, 71
of god, 74
importance of, 69
interracial, 81
Joseph Smith and, 20,
32
sealing ceremony and,
69, 70
*see also* polygamy
McKay, David O., 88
Melchizedek priesthood
founded, 28
membership, 29–30, 31
missionary work and,
90
revelations about, 17,
28–29
membership
Brigham Young and,
43, 64
current, 96
growth in
early, 18
from 1967–1977, 94
persecution and, 21,
37
recent, 7–8
*Meridian Magazine*, 85,
87
Methodist Church, 86, 87
Mexican-American War,
59
migrations
from England, 86
from Europe, 64

to Kirtland, 18, 19–20
to Nauvoo, 39–42
to Utah, 57–61
millennium, 23, 35–36,
37–38
missionary work
being called for, 89–90
commitment to, 84–85
Council of Seventy
and, 28
current, 7–8, 89
*Doctrine and Covenants*
and, 22
early, 64, 86, 87–88
endowment ceremony
and, 68
by families, 97
founding of Church of
Jesus Christ of
Latter-day Saints
and, 18
Golden Questions, 85,
87
to Native Americans,
80
public opinion about,
87–88
recruitment proce-
dures, 91–93, 94
rules for those doing,
93
success of, 94–95
targeting specific
groups, 95–96
in Tonga, 96–97
training for, 90–91
in twentieth century,
88, 90
types of missions,
88–89, 94–95
Missouri, 30, 38–39

*see also* Independence,
Missouri
Mormon (Nephite
leader), 24–25
*Mormon America* (Ostling
and Ostling), 65–66,
94
Mormonism
beliefs, 6, 42, 67, 98
about baptism,
27–28, 29
diverge from tradi-
tional
Christianity,
22–23
missionary work
and, 8
about plurality of
gods, 26–27
clannishness of
followers, 36
current opinion of
non-Mormons
about, 36
founded, 9
preferred terms for
followers of, 67
Moroni
initial appearances of,
14–15
material in Book of
Mormon by, 25
move to Ohio and, 18
return of plates to, 17
Mullen, Robert, 48, 75
mysticism, 10

name extraction program,
83
National Association for
the Advancement of

Colored People
(NAACP), 83
Native Americans
Book of Mormon and,
14, 17, 24
migration to Utah and,
60
relationship with,
80–81
Nauvoo, Illinois
charter, 54
conflicts in, with non-
Mormons, 46–48,
49, 50, 54
move from, 56–61
move to, 39–42
prosperity of, 46, 50
temple in, 51, 54
*Nauvoo Neighbor*
(newspaper), 41, 57
Nephites, 24–25
New York, 89

Old Testament
polygamy in, 33, 34
similarities of, to Book
of Mormon, 24, 25
Ostling, Joan, 45, 65–66,
94
Ostling, Richard, 45,
65–66, 94

Palmyra, New York, 11
Patriarch, 28
Pawnee (tribe), 60
peculiar people, 6
plural marriage. *See*
polygamy
Polk, James K., 59
polygamy, 32–35
Brigham Young and,
44, 46, 54, 66

Emma Smith and, 45
end of Church of Jesus
Christ of Latter-day
Saints recognition
of, 66
Joseph Smith and, 20,
32
opposition to
Mormon, 49, 53
non-Mormon,
46–47, 54, 63–64
oral preaching of, 42
power of women and,
35
Reorganized Church of
the Latter Day
Saints and, 55, 56
statehood and, 63–64,
66
Pratt, Orson, 18–19
Pratt, Parley, 18
Preparation Day, 94
Presiding Bishopric, 31
priesthoods
African Americans
and, 81
organization of, 29–31
Relief Society and, 72
revelations about, 17,
28–29
Primitive Methodists, 86
Prophet, the. *See* Smith,
Joseph
public opinion
about baptism of
deceased non-
Mormons, 83
about Book of
Mormon, 18
current, 36
membership growth
and, 37

about missionary work,
87–88
about move to
Kirtland, 19–21
about polygamy,
46–47, 54, 63–64
about Smith, 18, 19–20
sympathy for
persecution of
Mormons and, 41
violence and, 38–39,
47–48, 49, 50, 54

Quorum of the Twelve.
*See* Council of Twelve
Apostles

racial policies, 80–81, 83
Relief Society of Women,
45, 71–72, 80–81
Remini, Robert, 16
Reorganized Church of
the Latter Day Saints
(RLDS), 24, 35,
54–55, 56
revelations
from apostles, 17
about Church of Jesus
Christ of Latter-day
Saints operations,
20, 53
from Elijah, 27
First Vision, 12–13
from John the Baptist,
17, 28, 30
about migration to
Utah, 60
from Moroni, 14–15,
18, 25
about polygamy, 33
about priesthoods, 17,
28–29

revivalism, 9–10, 11
Richards, Willard, 49, 62
Rigdon, Sidney, 18,
    52–53, 54

Salt Lake City, Utah, 7,
    61–62, 70
seagulls, 60
sealing ceremony, 69, 70
Second Coming, 23,
    35–36, 37–38
secrecy, policy of, 32, 68,
    78
seer-stones, 14, 15, 16
Shupe, Anson, 79, 94
slavery, 66
Smith, Emma Hale
    (wife), 45
    Brigham Young and,
        55, 56
    marriage of, 15
    polygamy and, 72
    translation of Book of
        Mormon and, 16
Smith, Hyrum (brother),
    13, 49
Smith, Joseph
    assassination of, 49–51
    authority of, 18, 27, 29,
        42, 46, 48
    background of, 9–12
    banking violations by,
        39
    Book of Abraham and,
        26
    Brigham Young and,
        20, 43, 44, 51
    declared himself to be
        the Prophet, 20
    Doctrine and Covenants
        and, 22

marriages of, 20, 32–35
on missionary work, 84
Nauvoo conflicts and,
    47, 48
non-Mormon opinion
    about, 18, 19–20
Relief Society and, 72
revelations of
    from apostles, 17
    about Church of
        Jesus Christ of
        Latter-day Saints
        organization, 20
    from Elijah, 27
    First Vision, 12–13
    from John the
        Baptist, 17, 28, 30
    from Moroni,
        14–15, 18, 25
    translated Bible, 23–24
    translated Book of
        Mormon, 14, 15–16
Smith, Joseph, Sr.
    (father), 10, 12, 14, 15
Smith, Joseph, III (son),
    55–56
Smith, Lucy Mack
    (mother), 10, 11–12, 13
Smith, Samuel (brother),
    13, 44, 87
Smith, Sophronia (sister),
    13
Smith, William (brother),
    58
stake missions, 88–89
Stark, Rodney, 94–95
Supreme Court, 95

Tabernacle Choir, 70, 93
Taylor, John, 22, 49
Taylor, Zachary, 63–64

teenagers, 28, 41, 69
temples
    in East Germany, 96
    importance of, 31–32,
        42
    in Kirtland, 32, 39
    in Nauvoo, 51, 54
    policy of secrecy and,
        32
    in Salt Lake City, 62,
        70
temple sealings, 69, 71
Territorial Gazette
    (newspaper), 40
Thompson, Roger, 55–56
Thummim, 14, 15, 16
tithing, 76–77, 78
Tonga, 96–97
tongues, speaking in, 44
tracting, 94, 95
Twelve, the. See Council
    of Twelve Apostles

Urim, 14, 15, 16
Utah
    locusts and, 60
    migration to, 57–61
    Mormon population
        in, 7
    settlement, 61–62
    statehood, 63–64, 65,
        66
    temple in, 70
    territorial government,
        64, 65–66
Utah War, 66

Ward Teacher's Message
    (magazine), 79
Whalen, William, 88
Whitmer family, 18

Wiley, Peter, 69

Winter Quarters, 59–60, 61

women
  endowment ceremony and, 68
  family role of, 69, 71, 72, 73
  missionary work and, 90, 93
  polygamy and power of, 35
  religious limitations placed upon, 27, 71–72
  Reorganized Church of the Latter Day Saints and, 56

Woodruff, Wilford, 35, 66

work ethic, 76

Works, Miriam, 43, 44

Young, Brigham
  background of, 43–44
  *Doctrine and Covenants* and, 22
  Emma Smith and, 45, 55, 56
  government of Utah Territory and, 64, 65–66
  Joseph Smith and, 20, 43, 44, 51
  Kirtland temple and, 32
  leadership of Church of Jesus Christ of Latter-day Saints and, 52–54, 62–63
  membership growth and, 43, 86
  move west and, 57–61
  polygamy and, 44, 46, 54, 66
  racism of, 66, 81
  Reorganized Church of the Latter Day Saints and, 54–55
  revelations of, 60
  speaking in tongues by, 44

Young, Elizabeth (daughter), 43, 44

Young, John (father), 43

Young, Naby Howe (mother), 43

Young, Phineas (brother), 43–44

Young Gentlemen and Ladies Society, 41

Zion, 21, 35

# Picture Credits

# About the Authors

A former editor of children's books in New York City, Corinne J. Naden also served four years in the U.S. Navy as a journalist. She has written more than eighty books for children and lives in Tarrytown, New York.

A native New Yorker who lives in Brooklyn, Rose Blue has published some eighty fiction and nonfiction books for children. Two of her books were adapted for young people's specials aired by the NBC television network.